INSIDE RECUITING™

THE MASTER GUIDE TO SUCCESSFUL COLLEGE ATHLETIC RECRUITING

VOLUME I

Stephen J. Brennan, Editor

Peak Performance Publishing
Omaha, Nebraska

Other Resources by Stephen J. Brennan:

The Recruiter's Library – audio and video recruiting materials
for coaches, parents, and student-athletes.

Library of Congress Catalog Card Number: 97-75699

International Standard Book Number: 0-9619230-8-3

Printed in the United States of America

10   9   8   7   6   5   4   3   2   1

Published and distributed by:
Peak Performance Publishing
A Division of Peak Performance Consultants, Inc.
14728 Shirley Street
Omaha, Nebraska 68144-2144 U.S.A.
(800) 293-1676

DEDICATION

To all college athletic coaches
and administrative recruiters worldwide.

TABLE OF CONTENTS

FOREWORD

I am very excited and honored to be writing the Foreword to this book. College recruiting in the 1990's has taken on a life of its own, it seems. Recruiting services have arisen literally overnight in some cases and it seems like fans all over the country want to know who "their" university has signed. Recruiting has become a very secretive process to many coaches who recruit high school athletes today. But it doesn't have to be that way.

For years, college coaches have been recruiting student-athletes without any kind of guidelines or education of the recruiting process. No one shared ideas, even within the university athletic staff. If you wanted to know how to recruit, you needed to learn it alone. But finally, Steve Brennan and his staff have come to the aid of college recruiters nationally with this outstanding book.

Inside Recruiting™: The Master Guide to Successful College Athletic Recruiting – Volume I is a precedent-setting publication. It is the only book of its kind anywhere that professionally discusses the strategies and techniques of some of the top college recruiters around the nation. In no other book will you find articles on such critical recruiting topics like organizing home and campus visits, how to work with the high school coach, how to recruit on a minimal budget, and how to handle negative recruiting. We coaches are very thankful that Steve and his staff have made such a valuable recruiting resource available to us.

Coaches from all levels of competition, including NCAA Divisions I, II, and III, NAIA, and junior college can all take advantage of the information in this book. Recruiters in both men's and women's programs can all gain an insight or two from this book. And the exciting part of this book is that it is the first volume of the *Inside Recruiting™* **Series** that Steve has developed. Coaches can take advantage by ordering Volume II which will be available in January 1999.

Finally, this is a book that all college athletic recruiters need to read and have in their library. It is not a book that has all the answers, but it is a book that will assist all athletic recruiters by giving you an idea or two that you can implement into your program immediately. Steve Brennan and his staff have made a significant contribution to coaching education in this book, and I invite all coaches to take advantage of the information presented here. Sharing, not hiding information, is how the college recruiting process will improve.

— *Rod Delmonico*
Head Baseball Coach
University of Tennessee

INTRODUCTION

Welcome to Volume I of *Inside Recruiting™: The Master Guide to Successful College Athletic Recruiting.* The *Inside Recruiting™* Series may well be one of the most important pieces of recruiting literature for college athletic recruiters.

This book is being compiled to meet the need for written recruiting materials for college coaches. With the advent of **The Recruiters Institute™** and **The Recruiters Library™**, college coaches have the opportunity to stock their coaching libraries with an assortment of recruiting resources. Audio, video, recruiting lists and technology sources are currently available. However, no written literature has been available to college athletic and administrative recruiters…until now.

Each article in *Inside Recruiting™* is written by a highly successful college recruiter from a high-profile program. Coaches in Divisions I, II, III, NAIA and junior college can all benefit from the articles and hopefully take one or two ideas and implement them immediately into their own programs. The format of the articles makes for easy reading, and the larger type style will inhibit any eye problems from occurring.

Rod Delmonico, the highly successful baseball coach at the University of Tennessee, delivers a very positive message in the Foreword to college athletic recruiters. He mentions how college athletic recruiting has exploded over the past few years, and how recruiters need to have some guidelines and ideas regarding the recruitment of student-athletes today. Recruiters need to work hard to "sign" student-athletes to their school. College athletic recruiters will find *Inside Recruiting™* to be a most helpful resource.

Inside Recruiting™: The Master Guide to Successful College Athletic Recruiting – Volume I is the only book of its kind for college recruiters. Volume I contains a tremendous amount of extremely useful information. It is my hope that the *Inside Recruiting™* Series will be the primary resource for all college athletic and administrative recruiters when they need to find effective recruiting methods for today's want-it-all recruits.

— *Steve Brennan*

Acknowledgments

I want to sincerely thank my staff of Bridget and Jon for their professional handling of this project to its completion and to Gary Anderson at the University of Nebraska at Omaha for the use of the photo on the front cover. I am especially thankful to the wonderful coaches whose articles make up this book.

Finally, I want to thank my family, Lorna, Anne, Brad and Stephanie for their support, patience and encouragement in allowing Dad to complete this project.

RECRUITING THE ATHLETE FROM A TO Z

by Ceal Barry

There are a lot of details involved in recruiting the athlete from start to finish.

My assistant coaches got a big kick out of the fact that I'm sharing this information. I really am kind of an impostor, because they do the majority of the legwork when it comes to recruiting.

A large part of the credit for bringing good players to the University of Colorado has to do with the assistant coaches that I have. One thing that has helped us be successful in recruiting is that the assistant coaches have been in our program for a long period of time. I think that has helped us with continuity and understanding how to sell our program. Continuity among the staff definitely has been a factor in our recruiting.

Keys to Success

In college athletics, you must understand that recruiting is the lifeblood of your program. You have to recruit — or think about recruiting — every day, in some way, shape or form. If you think that you can recruit only in the off-season, and during the season you are only going to condition players, teach players and practice and have team meetings and academic meetings — that is an unrealistic expectation. As a coach, you really never get a day off. It doesn't matter if it's Thanksgiving, Christmas, Easter, or Valentine's Day. It doesn't matter. The more you think about it — the more you scheme, the more you plan, and the more you are involved with recruiting — the more successful you are going to be. That leads into my second fundamental concept — your work ethic.

First, you need to understand how important your work ethic is. Second, your work ethic definitely correlates to the number and the ability of the recruits that you get. I don't think it's all luck. I think you sign players because you work harder than other people. Along with the work ethic, you have to be enthusiastic about recruiting. I've been a head coach for 17 years and I would not say that I am the most outgoing of coaches. I'm not a comedian in home visits. As a matter of fact, I can tend to be a little bit shy. So my first perception of myself is that I'm not a good recruiter, because I'm a little bit shy. I don't like to go out there and walk up to people and introduce myself and that sort of thing.

I think I've become a better recruiter as I've *thought of myself* as a better recruiter. I think if you *think of yourself* as a good recruiter and are enthusiastic about the recruiting process, you're going to be a better recruiter.

The third key to success is that the head coach must be involved in the recruiting process. Minor sport coaches in Division II, Division III, NAIA or junior college don't particularly have that problem. But if you're Division I and you have a restricted earnings coach and two full-time assistants, your head coach had better be involved.

My assistants are trying to teach me how to use the computer. I turn on my computer and there's a message, "Ceal, write Jill and Shelly." It's on my computer. They put little sticky notes on my door or they put a message on my voice mail. They'll tell me who to write this week.

I have a tendency to start doing the "head-coaching" things — meet with players or check with the strength or conditioning coaches — or doing anything, except writing to potential recruits. My assistant coaches are very good at making me get involved. They'll even say, "Ceal, while you're busy watching the NBA playoff games, make sure that you jot Melody a note." They constantly remind me.

So if you are an assistant coach, make sure that your head coach is involved. I think that the player/coach relationship is significant in eventually signing the prospect.

Evaluating and Assessing Potential Recruits

> **"Know what the elements are that players need to be successful in your program."**

The first thing that we look at is athletic ability, as we evaluate a videotape or see a prospect in person. It's important for you to know what you want. What are the most important things a player needs to possess to be successful in your program? We like to play man-to-man defense. We play 40 minutes of man-to-man defense. So a big, slow player is not going to fit into our system, because we would sacrifice size for quickness.

If you're an assistant coach and you're new to the program, it's important to understand what your head coach values before you go out on the road and recruit. What an assistant coach considers a great player may not be what the head coach wants for his or her particular system. I tell my assistants that we value quickness. At Stanford, for example, three-point shooters might be a priority. At Colorado, quickness is a priority for us. We don't base our program around our offense; we base our program around our defense.

As you recruit, you look for things that you cannot teach. No matter how much time you put in, it's difficult to teach quickness. Obviously, you can't "teach" size either. Size is not going to change a whole lot. That's a second aspect. If you've already got a guard at a position who is shorter, smaller than the second guard that you're looking at the same position, you might want someone a little bit taller or stronger. But quickness is still an asset; that's something that's important. That has remained our number one criteria.

Basically, recruit the attributes in players that you cannot teach. The second consideration of athletic ability we look for is size; the third is skill. If a player meets those particular attributes athletically, the next thing that we look for is academic ability. This may not be important to you at your particular school. It often depends on what the coach values.

For me, at Colorado, I really value players who don't make mental errors. If you don't want your players out there making mental errors, then it's probably going to be in your best interest to recruit players who show some success academically. Academic achievement pretty much goes along with our team's philosophy.

I tell our players that if they're not successful academically, then it probably shows a lack of self-discipline. It probably shows a little lack of commitment, too. If you have a player who has been a 2.4 grade point average student in high school, you can't expect them to come into the collegiate level and be a 2.8. I've found it pretty much to be the other way around. If you're recruiting a student with a 2.8 at the high school level, they might be a 2.4 at the college level, at least at the University of Colorado.

I've found that in our academics at Colorado, the average ACT score in our College of Arts and Sciences for automatic admission is a 25. So a non-athlete student would not be admitted to our Arts and Sciences program unless they had a 25 on the ACT. If they were to try to get into the College of Business, it's 27; if they're in engineering, it would be a 29. What this means is when I go out to recruit and I see a player with a 19 ACT score and they're trying for admission into our College of Arts and Sciences, I think that they're probably already at a disadvantage. There are a certain number of A's that are going to be given out, a certain number of B's,

certain number of C's. It stands to reason that the person with the 19 ACT is going to get a good percentage of the D's.

I think you can recruit around potential problems. We're looking for players not only with tremendous athletic ability but with academic ability. I think when we value academic ability, we're going to eliminate problems before players ever get to the first day on campus.

Another thing that we look at is a player's emotional stability. It's important to evaluate their relationship with the coach. Wherever you evaluate a player in person or if you evaluate them on a videotape, it's important to carefully examine how they interact with their coach. If they're having a problem with their head coach at the high school level, that's pretty much a red flag that chances are they may have a relationship problem with their coach at the college level. When you're talking with prospects on the phone, when you have your first contact with them, if they lack respect for their parents, chances are they're going to lack respect for other people in positions of authority.

It is true that you can prejudge. You see a player and they have tattoos or four earrings or whatever the case may be and you make a decision, without even knowing that person. I think it's important not to prejudge.

I've had a player on my team who happened to be from the state of Colorado. In high school she had a tattoo, her hair was shaved on the sides and she had a blonde streak in it. If she had not been from the state, and if I had not been aware of her personally and had some contact with her because she had been on campus, I might have second-guessed my willingness to recruit her. But because I knew her and because she had been on our campus, I didn't prejudge her. She was recruited and was probably the hardest worker out of 15 players that we had on our team. So when you see tons of kids and you're evaluating the emotional aspect of prospects, I think it's important not to prejudge. It's possible that once you have the opportunity to get to know them, there's more to them than just what is on the surface.

What Things Can You Change?

Confidence is something that can be built. Immature players can mature. However, something that is difficult to change is selfishness. If you recruit a selfish player, I don't care how effective you are, it's like recruiting somebody with no speed. If you recruit someone with no speed, it's hard to make them quick. If you recruit a player who is selfish, you have to really be in tune to that fact. In a team sport, it's difficult to change selfishness. Sometimes, it's a confidence thing.

> "Some things you can change; others you can't. Know the difference between the two."

Some insecurities show out on the floor. Insecurity can change, especially when they're in a college environment and you help a player build confidence. With immaturity, they can mature, but selfishness is one that I've found in the past is difficult to change. Once you recruit a selfish player and you've made that commitment, they're on your team and they have the potential to ruin your team.

Once you've evaluated all those things and you like this player, you decide that this is the player. You had better like them, if you're going to recruit them. Isn't it easier to recruit when you like the player? The worst thing to do is have a kid on your list that you're going to call or write and you don't like them. It doesn't particularly motivate you to sit in your office at night and make a phone call, if you don't like them. They might be great players, but I think you have to get a connection with a player early on.

For example, I had one player in particular that I really enjoyed talking to. That motivated me to want to get to know her better. As soon as I got her on the telephone and had the opportunity to talk with her, then I liked her a little bit more. It's important to evaluate very clearly all the important things — I like the fact she's a good player or he's a good player; I like the fact that she or he is a good student; I like her/his personality; I like the way this player

> **"Be sure to factor in *personality*. You'll be spending a lot of time with your players."**

interacts with his or her teammates on the floor. Now, step one of the evaluation process is completed. Now you're motivated to recruit. Now you want to sell your program to them. You want them to like you, because you like them.

What Are The Odds?

The fourth thing that you have to do in the evaluation process is evaluate whether you have a chance to recruit a player. We're out in Boulder, Colorado. I've seen great players in Alabama. I don't think that we have a very good shot at getting a player from Alabama. I've seen players in Southern California. We're recruiting against PAC 10 schools, but I think we can get them away from Southern California. I've seen great players in Texas. I know from experience that we can recruit a player from Texas. How do I know?

Certain things will tell me if a player can be recruited. First, do they return your questionnaire? Second, do they answer the phone when you call — when their mom says you are on the phone and they're sleeping or in the shower or whatever? It only takes one or two phone calls and that pretty much is an indicator.

I don't necessarily think that we should take the high school coach's word for granted all the time. This is something else to evaluate. It might be the player's summer coach. High school coaches are usually a little bit more in tune. People have different agendas. You need to find out straight from the horse's mouth — what does the player actually think? How interested is this player in your program?

After we've evaluated our recruits, our secretary puts the players' names in the computer. My assistants and I have it all computerized. We group them. If they're a top recruit, we call them "money." We have three digits that we put next to our recruits. If they're topnotch, they're labeled as "money sign 97." That doesn't mean we're giving them money, so don't misunderstand me. That means that they're "money in the bank," so to speak. If we sign them, they're going to be able to make a contribution to Colorado's program. They're a "money" player.

We have index cards that we use to evaluate players when we go on the road.

We collect information on that card, including:

- name
- contact information
- attitude
- size
- how they interact with their coach
- how they interact with their teammates
- address
- athletic ability
- their quickness
- shooting range

Then we have groupings. If they're a "Money 97" player, they're top of the line. If they're "2-96," that means they're second in line. If they're "HIS", (and I hate to admit this) that means they're history. They will never be recruited by the University of Colorado.

Sometimes we have players with tremendous athletic ability, tremendous academic ability, great emotional stability, but they have absolutely no interest in coming to CU. They are also labeled "history." We're not going to put any more time or effort into them. They go into what some people call the inactive file — to us they're history; we won't see them again.

What Is It About First Impressions...

The first contact then becomes important. Before the NCAA rules changed, if you had not contacted a senior-to-be during their junior year, it was a hopeless case. Now, with the rules change — the limited number of evaluations, no phone calls until July first of their senior year — you can get in on a player just prior to their senior year. I wouldn't have said that maybe three or four years ago.

> "It really is true: You never get a second chance to make a first impression."

I think it's been demonstrated that late contact is still effective. We have quite a few players with whom we've made a first contact in June, July or August prior to their senior year. If it's past July first prior to their senior year, and you're able to make a phone call, I would make that call right away and get either the player or the parents on the telephone.

That first phone call is critical. If the head coach can make the first contact on the telephone with the senior-to-be, that's probably going to make even more of an impression. I can't emphasize enough that the head coach needs to be involved. If you really want this player, then you've got to have your head coach making those phone calls.

It's important that we find out the correct spelling of player names, parents' names, correct addresses, and all those things. Don't rely on the AAU program or what was sent back in the questionnaire or anything. I would check spelling for everything so that when you begin writing to prospects, you've got an accurate name, address and home phone number.

It's also important to find out the family situation. Are they living with their real father and real mother or are they living with a stepfather and real mother or is there no father? More often than you may think, they may be living with their high school coach. The mother might live in town but they may be living in a guardianship. It's important to find this out.

Sometimes the player's last name is Smith, the mother's last name is Jones, and the father's last name is Brown. Don't make the mistake of addressing a mailing to Mr. and Mrs. Brown, when the mother is Mrs. Jones. That's happened before.

Details are important.

If you care, if you want to sign the player, it's important to find out the correct address. It may sound like a little thing, but let's say you have two mailings and you address them incorrectly, while the University of Nebraska, for example, addresses their mailing correctly. We're already a step behind. Find out nicknames. One of the worst things that you can do is call a player Teresa on the phone over and over again, and then discover that all the other coaches and all the other colleges are calling her by her nickname, "T". They know the nickname and *nobody* calls her Teresa except the University of Colorado. Find out if she has a nickname. Find out if she goes by her middle name. These little things breed familiarity between you and the recruit.

> "Remember, the little things – like spelling a player's name correctly – mean a lot."

If the third contact is prior to July first of their senior year or if it's after September first of their junior year, and your first contact is written, it's important that the communication be personal. We have all but eliminated form letters in our program.

If they are a "Money 97," "Money 98" or "Money 99" at Colorado, they should not receive a form letter. Now there are certain limitations — on sophomores, especially. You can't send personalized letters. But for a junior, as of September first of their junior year, all correspondence should be handwritten.

You may be limited in your staff, but if there are players you really want and you're sending form letters to them and your opponent is sending handwritten letters to them (individually addressed and handwritten), your opponent is going to have an edge.

In our first contact we may hand write the letter and give her all the information that we possibly can about the University of Colorado. We also enclose a questionnaire in the first contact letter. With the questionnaire it would be worth your time and the expenditure to have a postage paid return envelope. This is going to depend on your budget. But if you want the questionnaire back, I'd make it as easy as possible for them to get it back to you. We include a postage paid return envelope so they can send the questionnaire back to us. They don't have to worry about addressing it or finding postage. I think you get a better rate of return on the questionnaire when it's low-hassle.

As I've told my assistants, the fact that a prospect did not return the questionnaire does not necessarily mean that they're not interested. If it's a tremendous prospect and they're being recruited and they've gotten 100 letters and questionnaires, we might be the 99th to send our questionnaire. Just because they didn't send the questionnaire back doesn't necessarily mean that they're not interested.

> **"Keep a paper trail of everything you've sent out, so you know what you've said."**

We photocopy everything that goes out of our office. We create a file for every player we want. We don't correspond with our second-tier prospects as often. If I write a handwritten note and I enclose whatever I'm allowed to enclose these days, I make a copy. I want to know what I've sent. I create a file and we clip the questionnaire on the left side of the folder so that we have all the information on the left side. We date all correspondence chronologically, so we have a copy of everything that we have sent out. This is mainly so that when I'm sitting out in the car or in a restaurant before I go for the home visit, I can review everything we have written to the prospect in the last year.

I think the worst thing is to have told a player one thing and then you sit down during the home visit and tell her another thing. You need to know what you said a year ago or what you said six months ago. You can't refer to her dog, Spot, in a letter and then go in and ask what her dog's name is. If you photocopy everything, you'll be better organized.

The bottom line when it comes to closing the deal is credibility. All throughout the recruiting process, creating trust and credibility is of utmost importance. And this definitely comes from the head coach.

Keeping in Touch

After the first contact, whether our prospect is a junior or a senior, we write our recruits once a week. We may write to the prospect or to the parent. This is why it's so important that you know if the parents are living together, if they have separate addresses, or if the parents' last names are different, and what the relationship is with the parent. You may have mom and stepfather in one home with the player and you may have the real father in another state.

In our mailings, there are certain things that we "hit" or emphasize more. Some of the things you probably hit are your facilities, your strength and conditioning program, your academic advising, attendance, and your conference. When Colorado changed from the Big Eight to the Big 12 conference, one of our mailings explained who was coming into our conference. We started recruiting a little more in Texas. It made sense for us to educate parents and prospects in Texas about the fact that we would be in Texas in the future and that Texas and Texas Tech were on our schedule.

This information is covered in a weekly mailing and it is handwritten. Keeping up with the rules is up to my assistants, but they have certain enclosures that go with each mailing. But everything is handwritten and everything is photocopied, so that we know if we have already told her about our strength and conditioning program, tutorial support, or sports medicine program. The mailings for weeks one, two and three may be sent to the recruit. But the fourth week, we're going to write the parents. Then week five, we go back to the recruit. We don't write the high school coach or the junior college coach on a weekly basis.

Most of our contact with those particular people are on the telephone, though they do receive what we would consider occasional mailings, media guides, camp brochures, etc.

Stand Out from the Crowd

Obviously if we're writing to our recruits, we're writing on notecards or stationery. We've got four different types of scenic note cards. We chose one scene showing when Colorado had a sell-out crowd. One of the things we like to sell is the beauty of our campus in Boulder, so we have one notecard with a scene of the campus with mountains. We have one with a Colorado buffalo on the front.

> **"Consistency and uniqueness can set you apart from the rest of the recruiting crowd."**

Once you have a note card made up, if you reprint it without changes, it's cheaper every time that you have it printed up. We've had the same note cards since 1989. We *can* change the inside of the card. We never put my name or my assistant coaches names in the cards, so that we can use them over and over. We never date it. It's basically generic information inside. One message says "Colorado's commitment to excellence." Another says "Colorado Big Eight Champions, 1989, 1993." Another is blank inside.

The way I look at it, you have a certain amount of money in your recruiting budget and priorities for your program. I'm going to do a lot of traveling in July and I need to make home visits in September and we need to evaluate throughout the school year. You need to look at your budget and determine what percentage of your budget you are going to use for note cards to help sell your program.

During the junior year, you're limited on the number of times that you can actually go out and see recruits. On the other hand, you're not limited in the number of times you can write them. So I would spend some money and take some time to design, or have someone else design, some note cards that help you sell your program and your campus in whatever way is legal and in whatever colors you can use. Your competitors are out there using attractive note cards. You want the recruit going to the mailbox to notice your particular piece of correspondence.

Reach Out and Touch Someone

July 1st, prior to their senior year (for basketball — I'm not quite sure for the other sports), it's important again for the head coach to make telephone calls. We make a list each week. We're allowed to bring 12 players to campus. I might have a list of 10 prospects, if we need to sign three. My assistants give me a list of 10 that I need to call every week. I might call them all the first two or three weeks. By that point, they're getting a little tired of me, so I'll suggest that an assistant coach call them next time. Then I go back and make the calls the following week. The majority of the conversations the recruits have are with the head coach.

> **"Make sure your telephone call isn't just a one-way conversation."**

I can't make too many telephone calls in one night. If you have a list in front of you and you decide "I'm going to go 15 minutes with this one and get it done, then 15 minutes with this one and get it done," you won't have quality conversation. If you have the mentality that you want to get it over with, you want to go home, that's not a positive way to approach calls, and it will come through in your voice.

I think it's important not to call too many recruits in one night. You've got to be a judge of how much emotion and how much enthusiasm you have. Maybe two is your limit, depending on the length of the calls. If you feel yourself getting tired and you're thinking that you just want to get one more out of the way, that's probably not a good approach to making the phone call. I'd wait until the next night or the next day and go into the phone call with a lot of enthusiasm and a lot of interest.

I look at the list and I see who I can get ahold of. If the conversation is rolling — I don't know if it's any different with guys than with girls — but if it's going well and they're willing to talk, if they want to talk for an hour, I'll talk for an hour. It usually doesn't go any longer than that. Sometimes the conversation is 10 minutes. But you have to have an agenda for your call. We have a notepad right there for us to take notes on including everything that is said on the phone. In the telephone portion of your recruiting, it's important to ask them questions and get them to talk.

In the first phone contact, I've found the players are usually intimidated or shy. They don't say too much. So you're looking for things to say. Try and create questions that don't result in yes and no answers. If you ask, "Are you willing to go away from home?," they may say "yes" and that's it. Use open-ended questions, such as, "How do you feel about going away from home?" Then you give them an opportunity to talk.

Working Against the Negatives

There two things that are constantly used against us in recruiting. Everybody thinks, "Oh, how easy it must be to recruit to Colorado." Let me tell you, we're not exactly surrounded by metropolitan areas. We recruit in Dallas, San Antonio, Kansas City, Los Angeles, and San Francisco. We're surrounded by Utah, Wyoming, Arizona, Western Nebraska, Western Kansas, New Mexico. We don't have a big population base surrounding Boulder and Denver, Colorado. We have to go out.

The two things that are used against us are the distance and the geography, and also that it is so cold in Colorado. Everybody has a perception; our opponents create the perception that it's like Alaska in Boulder. We attack that right from the beginning. Within the second to third phone call, I go ahead and ask them, "So what do you think about going away from home?" "Well, you know, I could probably do it." So we'll talk about that. Eventually, down the line in the recruiting process, I've already spoken to the recruits about it. I've already told them that we have a major airport in Denver and I've told them that Boulder is 20-25 minutes away.

> **"You have to be able to turn a negative into a positive in your prospect's mind."**

I think it's important that you understand what your opponents are going to use against you and challenge those things. We recruit Southern California. Recruiters from USC, UCLA, Arizona and Arizona State are going to say, "Why do you want to go to Colorado and live in an igloo? Why do you want to go out there where it snows all the time?"

Sometimes it's kind of funny, because I've had players come from California or Texas who hope that it snows when they come to make their visit, because they've never seen snow. Of course, I hope it doesn't snow too much.

Find out what prospects want. Find out what their needs are. Find out what their interests are. It's important to gather as much information as possible in the first six weeks of your phone calls.

Avoid Phone Tag and "Ping Pong Phone"

Another area of concern in recruiting is getting recruits to call you back. We tried one method and then rejected it because it was bouncing recruits around the office. We were trying to make it interesting for the prospect. I would talk to them and then bounce them over to Barb, my assistant. She would talk to them and then transfer them over to Jan. All of a sudden, they feel like they're just a ping pong ball being bounced around the office.

I think it's more effective if you can get an 800-number and have recruits call back to visit with a particular coach. Say to the recruit, "Coach Smith isn't here right now, but she really wanted to talk to you. She'll be in tomorrow and wants to know when she can call you. Would it be possible for you to call her back?"

It's not so much that Coach Smith has a whole lot to say, but it's getting recruits familiar with your program so that they have the sense that they're welcome to call your office. You may need them to be in touch in November or right prior to the signing date. You may need them to call you but if they have never called your office, they may feel uncomfortable about making the call. Let's say you talk to them on Sunday and they're making their decision on Tuesday. By Tuesday night you haven't heard from them. If they have never called your office, I think the chances of having them call you back are less.

Get them in the habit as soon as possible. They don't need to call you every week. Don't limit yourself to once a week just because the rules say that. They're allowed to call you back; it's legal.

Tailoring Your Visits

Home visits are really your first opportunity to sit down with recruits face to face and discuss the program. The home visit and the campus visit may be the most critical aspect of the recruiting.

> **"Home and campus visits may be the most critical part of your recruiting."**

Your appearance is important. You need to gauge, am I going to a farm or the suburbs? I recruited a player who lived on a 2500 acre farm. During the home visit, I ended up slopping through the mud, looking at pigs and calves. I wasn't appropriately dressed. My most critical decision prior to making the visit to this player was "What do I wear?" If I wear jeans and tennis shoes and a sweater, they're going to think I'm a slob. If I dress up nice, they're going to think I'm a fool. So I was trying to decide on changing clothes from the airport to the farm about three times.

Appearance is definitely important. You need to put your best foot forward. You're a salesperson. You're trying to sell your school. The window to your school is you. When you walk into the door, it's important that you wear clothes that travel well. I understand it's trivial, but I wouldn't walk in the door for a home visit and not look the part. If you want to sell your school and you want the image of your school to be represented well throughout your home visit, you don't want that recruit looking at you and saying, "He's got a grease spot on his tie." That's happened before.

Another thing to remember is that recruits talk to other recruits. They want to know what the coach had on. It's the littlest thing, the smallest detail. You think that recruits are making their decision based on your computer program or on your psychology program. A lot of times they base their decision on how they *feel* about you. Your appearance is the first thing they see. I'm not saying that it's the most essential part of the sales pitch, but when you walk into the door and sit down, how you carry yourself, your confidence, your courtesy, your attention, your listening to family members, knowing the family members names, being well informed, and just your entire presence in their living room — all of this is important.

I have made it a point to get to the kitchen table in home visits. I do everything that I can to get out of the living room situation. I have a lot of little visual aides. I like to throw things around. One of the things that sells at Colorado are the mountains, so I have a lot of pictures of mountains. You can't leave those things with them. Color photographs, postcards are not legal anymore. However, it is important for prospects and parents to see what our campus looks like because it is one of our biggest selling points.

> **"Make your home visit an interactive experience, not a lecture or a boring presentation."**

If I have to stand up and walk over here from the couch, it's easier for me on the kitchen table. I'm sitting here and I have mom here, dad here, and the recruit here and if the coach is on my side, I have him real close to me. Where you sit is important. If you're going by yourself and you've got all the attention, that's fine. If you have an assistant with you, you don't want yourself and your assistant sitting side by side preaching to the family. You want a situation where there's interactive communication.

You don't want intensity or tension during the visit. I think it's important to have a plan and important to be structured. I can get through all the material in the home visit in an hour if I talk from start to finish, which I hope not to do. I'm hoping that I'm asking enough questions, I'm getting enough interaction. If you end up lecturing to them, pretty soon they're looking at their watches or they've got homework to do, or they start taking phone calls.

When A Picture's Worth A Thousand Words, Why Are You Still Talking??

We have a few visual aids. One of the things that has been most successful for us is a notebook with pictures. If the parents cannot make the campus visit, I want to bring the campus to them. You can do that through a recruiting film. The admissions office may have a film, or a highlight film of ability, of action, that sort of thing. But the parents want to know a little bit more about the campus. They want to know about the dorms. They want to know who's in a room with whom. They want to know how close the dorms are to the campus. We've invested in 8x10 pictures; we put them in a regular 3-ring binder with plastic covering for each of the pictures. I put them in chronological order to go along with my outline, so I've got pictures to show them. If they're bored with my presentation and don't want to listen, at least they can look.

I have a packet of information that I leave with them, but I usually don't go through the packet. In case they want to know about playing time or returning players, I always have a list of the roster and last year's statistics. I leave them that information.

If I have an area of weakness in my presentation, it's that it tends to be too structured. You want some structure, you want planning, you want organization. You want to leave them thinking that you really know what's going on. On the other hand, you want them to feel that you're a pretty nice person. This is the school where their son or daughter is going to go play.

I think at some point, you chuck the plan. If I'm going to be in a home two hours, I set aside one hour for all the details, all the questions. Are we going to pay for her fifth year if she blows out a knee? Who is she going to room with? How do you travel? Then I leave plenty of time so we can talk about what really counts. Are you going to take care of my daughter? Are you going to take care of my son? That's what really counts. But take care of the details first. They may interrupt you after 30 minutes. They don't want to hear any more details. They just want to know about you. They want to know, if I send my son or my daughter to your university, what's going to happen. They want to know all the things that could happen at the collegiate level. You have to assure them that you're going to be there and that you care about their son or daughter. When players walk on your campus, you're the surrogate mother or surrogate father, but you're going to care for them just like they would.

> **"Be sure to allow enough time for questions from the prospect and his or her parents."**

When They Come To You

Before a prospect makes a campus visit, talk to your players. It's important to educate your players on how to act on a campus visit. They've been through the recruiting process and they liked it; that's why they came. I used to be real hesitant to discuss campus visits with my players. It's kind of a touchy situation because you're recruiting people to compete with them. In the last two to three years I've been much more candid with my players.

For each recruit that we bring into campus, we have an extensive itinerary. We really encourage parents to come. It might be more work for you; you might be occupied with the parents from Friday at 3:00 p.m. to Sunday at 11:00 a.m. and your kids might be occupying your recruits and some of the things will overlap. But I think it's important that you bring the parents to campus if you can. They have to pay for it. You're limited in what you're allowed to pay for, but if you can get them on your campus I think you can make the sale, you can close the deal. Not necessarily right there, but if you've got mom and dad you're going to be able to point out some positives to them.

Your players become an important tool. I guilt trip them a little, and I admit it. I say, "Look, I've been working on this recruit for 15 months and it's down to Colorado, Washington, Iowa, and Wisconsin. She's making four campus visits. If we don't get her, we'll play against her." These are the things that are important.

The other motivation I use for my players is that we bring as many recruits as we can in September and October. I tell my players, "We need to recruit three players this year and if we can get it done by November, we're going to have a better season." So now they are involved. You have to sell your players on recruiting as well as you sell your staff on it.

It's important to have meals with your team, with the recruits, with the parents. I go in the cafeteria with the team, the players, and the parents so they can see how the team reacts with the coach. I think mom and dad want to see that. Can the players talk to the coach? Do they avoid her? Sit down with her? When we bring a recruit to campus, we go to lunch in the cafeteria with the player and sit down and talk.

> **"Get your players involved in recruiting prospective players during visits."**

It's important during the campus visit that the head coach and the recruit get some one-on-one time. Not head coach, recruiting hostess; not head coach, mom and dad and recruit; not head or assistant; just one-on-one, head coach and the potential player. If you want the player and you've worked for 12 months to bring them in, and all of a sudden you get them to campus and they go here and you go there, you're missing a great opportunity.

You're the person who has sold them, the person who has recruited them, the person who has been right by their side from the start. You need to be there to continue to sell during the campus visit. It takes a lot of time. That's one thing I said in the very beginning. Your work ethic makes a difference.

I remind my players that we're probably going to have six recruiting weekends. Be ready to sacrifice six of your weekends. Whether it's taking them to the football game, going on a campus tour, or introducing them to the athletic director, I want to know what people are saying. So I'm there. When they go back home and I'm on the phone with them, I want to be able to say, "Remember what our strength and conditioning coach had to say?"

The emphasis on the head coach is not meant to minimize the involvement of the assistant coaches. The assistant coaches set the table. The head coach has to close the deal.

Closing the deal means getting them to sign that letter of intent. If you wait for them to make the decision, if you wait for them to call you with their decision, you're probably going to lose. This is difficult on the telephone. If you have rules that are a little bit more lenient, you can do it face to face. Timing is important. Find the right time to bring it up. I'm not a high pressure salesperson. It doesn't fit my personality. You have to recruit your personality, just like you coach your personality. You need to get a commitment well before the deadline, at least seven days out.

If you're waiting, you're really gambling. Usually they're not going to make their decision until they visited all the campuses. If you're number one on their list, if the recruit has already told you you're number one, and they go to visit another campus, I already assume we're not number one any more.

If they visit another campus, get on the phone the night they get back and start rebuilding. It's all there, but you have to build it back up. Don't be afraid to call them. It's important when they get back that you call that night. It's important. You were number one; you get them back and then you can get that commitment.

In closing the deal, you've got to cover all the bases. Your credibility comes into play. The trust, the relationship that you have with the players, comes into play. You begin to bring up how far they'll be from home. "Well, it wasn't that important when we talked earlier. We already discussed that. You can get from St. Louis to Denver in two hours. We'll be playing at Missouri and your parents can drive there."

I'll say to them, "I really think, deep down in your heart, you really want to come to Colorado." They'll say, "Yeah, that's what I really want to do." By that point I already know whether I've lost them. I know if I have them. Then I'll say, "You know what you're having a hard time with? You're having a hard time with the coach at the other school. You don't know how to tell her that you don't want to go there." I'm usually right. My prospect will say, "She's going to give me 15 reasons why I shouldn't come to Colorado."

So we help her or him say no to that other school. Otherwise, if you leave it up to them and they really want to come, but they don't know how to say no to the other school, they might not say no. And all of a sudden you've lost them. Do your homework and set the stage and get the recruit set. And when you're sure, you help them commit. I think you'll be able to close the deal.

Author Profile: Ceal Barry

Ceal Barry is the head women's basketball coach at the University of Colorado. She has 18 years of college recruiting experience, has won conference, district and national coaching awards, and has coached USA Junior Select teams, USA Women's World Championships teams, Jones Cup teams and has been a member of the Olympic coaching staff.

MAXIMUM UTILIZATION OF THE HIGH SCHOOL COACH

by Barry Copeland

What percentage of your success as a coach do you think is attributed to recruiting? 90% percent or higher? 100% percent?

One of the reasons why recruiting is so important is because of the time demands that the NCAA has implemented, as far as number of contacts you can have with recruits and the time you can evaluate. Your ability to recruit is often dictated by time alone. You have to be able to be organized and take less time to do what, in the past, you had more time to do. My first full-time recruiting coordinator position was in the early 1980s. At that time we didn't have the same demands as far as cutbacks in time contacts and it was a little easier.

When I was at Wisconsin-Green Bay, a small, Division I school, if I worked hard, I sometimes had a chance to sign a prospect because I might have outworked some of the other, more well-known programs recruiting him. That's not always the case; however, time is of the essence — you have to be good at what you do in a shorter period of time. I think recruiting in the future will focus on being more effective in a shorter period of time — more so than it has ever been.

Recruiting is a Four-Step Process

I see the recruiting process as having four basic phases: identification, assessment, selection and selling. What I have found is that most of the recruiting responsibilities fall into one of these four categories.

Identification means determining who you are going to recruit. First, what are the needs of your program? For example, how many freshmen, sophomores, juniors, and seniors will you have in your program? Second, consider your style of play.

My experience has been entirely in the sport of basketball, but many of my experiences are relevant to all types of men's and women's sports.

In order to begin the identification process in the sport of college basketball, you need to start by looking at 100 to 150 different names. That doesn't necessarily mean you're going to recruit 150 kids, but you need a list of between 100 and 150 to start with.

In the assessment phase, you look at the prospects you've identified and then determine what your needs are and how the recruits meet your needs. I believe that the ability to match a prospect to your program's needs is the most important talent of a recruiter. It's all about the ability to assess talent. Your ability to evaluate talent is the most important, significant factor in your success as a recruiter. It's even more important than the selling process itself, in my opinion. If you think convincing a prospect to play for you is more important, remember that you may be selling your program to the wrong customer. The recruit needs to fit your needs, or he or she won't play. So first you need to identify a list of prospects to recruit and second, begin to evaluate those prospects in terms of a fit with your program.

Remember, too, that the number of contacts you can have with a prospect have been reduced and recruiting now not only requires talent but a lot of effort as far as when and how you make your contacts. I believe developing a contact system is an important part of a recruiter's responsibilities.

> **"When it's time to start recruiting, sell, sell, sell!"**

In the selection process, recruiters are basically trying to determine how prospects fit our need. Once we've identified potential recruits, we begin to assess their strengths and how they fit our needs, based on how they fit into our current needs and our philosophy. Look at the big picture and ask yourself, "Do they fit in?" Who you are not going to recruit is just as important as who you do recruit, maybe even more so.

Finally, you arrive at selling. Sell, sell, sell. We sell everything. It's your responsibility as a recruiter to identify and emphasize what's most important to that player. What is he or she looking for?

A Little at a Time

I feel recruiting is a little bit like shaving. If you don't do a little bit every day, you can wind up looking like a bum. As a recruiter, this thought has to be part of your mindset each day. Recruiting is an ongoing process, not a single event. Did you make a phone contact today? Did you send a letter out? Are you thinking about what you're going to do next? Do you have a contact plan established so you can use your time and energy most effectively within the NCAA rules?

The Role of the Coach in Recruiting

To help you become more efficient, you must create a network of support. Part of that network includes the prospect's coach — either on the high school or junior college level. Why is the role of coach so important? You can only contact an athlete a certain number of times and during a certain period of time during the year.

Oftentimes, the coach becomes a sounding board orally for you. Even if they're not actively involved in their player's recruiting process, they are still going to be a part of the process — taking phone calls, letting you know when the recruit is playing, who they are playing against, or how they are doing. Even if you are not talking to the coach directly, he or she is still involved.

From an academic standpoint, there is more and more research being done on the role of the coach in relation to the performance of the athlete. Because of the interest in coaching, and the growing interest in sports in our country, the role of the coach and his or her impact on the athlete is being examined. As a recruiter, you want to know what kind of impact the coach/player relationship actually has.

What's Your Style?

Recent research has shown that a coach's style has a significant impact on an athlete's satisfaction and enjoyment. How does that relate to your success as a recruiter? If you're recruiting an athlete who gets along well with the coach and has a good relationship with that coach, it can have a tremendous impact on how you work with that coach in the recruiting process.

The opposite may be true, too. If the prospect plays for somebody they don't really care for, or if the coach doesn't like them, that's powerful information. It can impact your whole perception of the recruit. Imagine if a terrific recruit doesn't get much playing time because of his poor relationship with his coach.

The Role of the Coach

The coach plays many different roles with athletes. The role may even change, depending on circumstances, timing, and a player's needs. The role can be that of a mother or father figure, or it can be nothing more than providing social support.

The coach's role could be that of a true friend. It might be a disciplinarian role, when the player lacks that kind of tough support in the home.

Coaches sometimes have an influence on a player's relationship with his or her family, friends, and significant others. That's important information to know as a recruiter.

What is the Family Influence?

If I know that the family, particularly the father or the mother, has a good or bad relationship with the coach, that can influence my recruiting. Maybe I won't mention to the coach that I've spoken with the player's parents, if I know there's a bad relationship there.

> **"Know how involved the prospect's parents are in the recruiting process."**

Through the coach I can sometimes obtain information or feedback about a player's relationships with other people and whether they're good or bad. I think as a recruiter, we must emphasize certain things, because time is valuable. I always want to learn everything I can about a player within the time constraints. I don't always use everything I learn, but I want to know it anyway.

I think it's more important to know what you don't have to know. Then you know what you *don't* have to focus on.

Assess Your Relationship With the Coach

> "Start by taking a look at how you currently relate to the prospect's coach."

It's important to evaluate and assess your relationship with the high school coach. How well do you relate to him or her? Are your interactions mostly positive or negative? Even if it's mostly negative, you still need to cultivate the relationship. If you have a negative relationship or one with little interaction, you still need to cultivate the coach. There will be coaches whose players you love to recruit just because the coach is great to work with. Then there are cases that are totally the opposite. You need to cultivate a relationship with every coach, on some level.

Who is the Decision Maker?

Recruiting success, in my opinion, is contingent upon determining who makes the decision regarding where the athlete attends school. Sometimes, in recruiting, I've spun my wheels. Working hard is great, but wasting my effort isn't effective. I need to direct my energy where it needs to be emphasized.

The most important thing a recruiter needs to find out is who is making the decision regarding where the student will play. It could be the athlete. It could be the mother or the father.

A friend might even have a great impact on where a person attends school. That's important to know.

One of the reasons why Christian Laettner went to Duke was because a close friend was on their baseball team down there. Certainly, the coach can have a great impact on the student's decision. The choice is ultimately up to each athlete, but the contributing decision-makers must also be identified.

Parental Influence Can Be A Key

When I was recruiting in Wisconsin, if a Division I player was a decent player, he or she usually chose to attend Marquette or Madison or go somewhere out of state. We didn't have much luck convincing recruits of the benefits of attending the University of Wisconsin-Green Bay. His or her parents have a particular kind of school in mind for their child.

On the other hand, we found that when we went into the inner city of Chicago, our recruiting was focused a little more differently. We might find a minority African-American family with a single parent, either mother or father, who has a big impact on where their child attends school. In recruiting male basketball players, we often found that a mother who was a single parent was the key decision-maker. Sometimes it was an aunt or a grandmother.

Many times the father was the key. Another thing I found out about Wisconsin players is that the coach became a little more significant in the decision-making process, simply because basketball wasn't as intense or at as high of a level as it was to some of the kids we recruited in other backgrounds, in other parts of the population. When no one at home was pushing the player in one direction or another, we found that the coach became much more significant.

In those cases, the family would ask the coach for feedback. They would ask, "What do you know about this program compared to this program?" or "What do you know about this coach?"

Find Out Who Makes the Decision

I think it's important that you ask the player, the coach and the family, "Who makes the decision?" Then ask it again. Ask as many different people, in as many different ways, as you can. The player may say, "My coach is going to be a big factor in where I go." If so, we're going to involve him.

Or a player might say, "My family is going to help me make this decision." That's powerful to know. Another athlete might tell you, "Well, my mom's going to be a big factor here. We're really close."

Whenever I heard, "my mom and I are really close and she'd like to see me stay close to home," I never forgot that. I didn't even have to write it down. You always remember that. Little inferences like that are powerful. Maybe more powerful than anything else you get out of recruiting.

When the coach is a factor, we need to take a look at whether it is an active role or more of a buffer role. What I mean by that is, sometimes the coach will be involved just to regulate the recruiting process. He'll take phone calls, he'll take messages, he'll return phone calls, he'll get back to the family and act as a liaison between you and the family or the recruit.

He may not have anything to do with the decision, but he will act as a buffer. This is particularly true if you recruit someone who is a pretty good player and he or she has a lot of people calling.

Look to the Coach to Provide Guidance, Not Facts

The other scenario involves a coach who is active in the selection process and whose opinion is being considered. They can sometimes give you information about things you need to know and want to know. The danger in just asking instead of investigating is that they are not always accurate.

> **"Different coaches have different roles to play in the recruiting process."**

I learned this firsthand when I was recruiting a player for Mercyhurst College in Pennsylvania. The coach gave us some feedback as to what the player's background was. He said the player's parents were separated, and that his father was living with another woman.

The father had a powerful influence on the kid. But his dad was one of those people who lived vicariously through their children. He was an ex-jock, a good player. The father's girlfriend went to Mercyhurst. I'm thinking, "I have an advantage, don't I?"

So we began involving the father's girlfriend in the recruiting process and tried to get feedback from her. The coach said he felt that she was going to be a factor.

> **"Even when you think someone has influence with the prospect, he or she may not."**

Trying to get the father and girlfriend to agree was another thing. To make a long story short, neither one had anything to do with the player's decision. The recruit wanted in his heart to play Division I the whole time. He didn't really want to say it because he knew what his dad wanted. Although his father probably thought he was good enough to play Division I ball, he wanted his son to go someplace and be "the man" right away.

The recruit ended up walking on at a Big East school. We offered him a scholarship, but he didn't want it. He turned down a lot of Division II schools to walk on at a Big East school.

You need to ask questions and determine how active the coach is in the decision-making process. Then find out if the information you're receiving is accurate. It's sometimes hard to find out. The only way you really can know is by developing good relationships and a certain amount of trust, which takes time. You don't always have that kind of time.

Considering the Coach's Perspective

Keep in mind the coach's perspective when you recruit. I think most coaches have the best interests of their players in mind. But sometimes, for example, if you have a coach who has never had a player recruited before, and it's their first real recruit, what happens? The coach becomes very excited. They think their player is the greatest player who ever lived. Sometimes they promote that individual's abilities more so than is probably realistic. And sometimes they even know they're doing that.

Once I was recruiting a Division II player for about a year. We didn't find out until very late in the recruiting process, about the time of the signing period, that he was playing with a steel rod in his back. We never knew it.

His coach never told us that. He told us everything else, but he never told us that. That's the kind of stuff you should know, isn't it?

I like to think of coaches as promoters. They'll promote their athletes, but in a selective way. Most of them only tell about a player's strengths. What you don't know is sometimes more important than what you do know.

Working with a "Controlling" Coach

There's another coaching phenomenon that I've noticed. That's the coaches who control the whole recruiting process and control where their players end up. In these cases, you need to have a good relationship with those coaches. These coaches are usually with traditional programs that have won over a period of time.

Sometimes even recognizing this relationship isn't enough to stop the cycle. Once I was recruiting a player who was playing for a coach who had a history of sending his players to Division I schools. I knew that. But we had an outside chance to sign this player because he was very good, and we had some ties into the program he was from.

We got in late in the season and didn't spend a whole lot of time recruiting him. We called him and sent letters once in a while. We didn't spend much time recruiting him. At the end of his season, the Division I signing period, he hadn't received an offer.

I waited two or three weeks, then brought him in for the campus visit. He still had no Division I offers. He and his father came to visit. His dad tells me, "Coach, I want him to come here to Mercyhurst." I'm in, right? The player then goes home.

Two weeks later, we still haven't heard anything. Shortly after that I received a phone call that a Division I school was going to make him a late offer. There was more to it. The high school coach had played for this Division I coach. So there are many little things you need to know about the coach's style that are important as you go about recruiting the players.

Can Education Outweigh Favoritism?

I always felt that you could bypass some of the favoritism, if you could educate them about your program. Educate them about your philosophy. Do they understand how difficult it is to play for you? Do they know there may be some adjust-

ment that is necessary for the athlete to play at your level?

It doesn't matter what division you're in, or what sport you coach. It's a difficult adjustment for players, in a lot of different ways — physiologically, psychologically, and emotionally. A player has to be pretty good to play at the college level. Some high school coaches don't know that. They may think they know it, but they don't know how good your program is or what level you are at. It requires patience on your part to educate them. Are you willing to do that?

Educate them about academics as well as athletics. Make sure that they understand how difficult your school is or what the standards are for academic achievement. This is especially important if your school has individual standards that are higher than the NCAA mandates.

Coaches need to understand that players have to achieve to that level, because many times a coach will say, "Yeah, he's good! He's struggling right now in sociology, but he'll be all right."

Research Into the Coach's Role in Recruiting

"Every coach has some influence on the recruit, whether it is obvious or not."

The coach's role in recruiting does make a difference. The statistics back me up. Every coach plays a role in the recruiting process. A study that I conducted a few years ago looked at a 20% population of schools that had won 50% of their games or more over a five-year period. There were about 75 total schools across NCAA Division I, II, and III. We found that the influence of the high school coach and the parents did play a part. In fact, it was one of the more significant roles as to why athletes select a school.

Playing time is also a factor. If you've asked yourself, "Do we really need to emphasize the significance or the role of the coach?" The answer is yes. Our findings have been supported through some similar studies in football and in basketball. The role of the coach *does* have some kind of impact on whether or not an athlete selects a particular school.

Where Does the Coach Fit In?

When we looked at identifying prospects, we found that personal observation was the most important criteria. To most of us, that's nothing new. We all want to observe for ourselves whether or not we think a player will fit in.

We're all different; we all look for different things. You have to find athletes who will play for you, and not somebody else. Talent is in the eye of the beholder, so to speak.

Next, your selection criteria might include the assessment by the coach, whether in junior college or high school. I used to fill out a form that included both subjective and objective information as a frame of reference. I always wanted to have too much information, rather than not enough. It seemed like the more information I obtained, the more I was able to determine what I did or did not have to focus on. I wasn't concerned about things such as attitude, work ethic, compatibility or hobbies. I wanted to know, are they coachable? That's the one thing I really wanted to know. Are they coachable? If they're coachable, they're probably all of the other things you're looking for, too.

Seek Out Regular Feedback

I developed a self-report, a little form that I put together for the coaches to rank their players on. You can gear it toward whatever you coach — baseball, basketball or field hockey. Just put the skills on there that are necessary, in your mind, to be successful in your particular sport, with ratings on a 1-5 scale.

> **"Get the coach involved by having him or her provide you with objective information."**

Have the coach give you some feedback. Where does the player fit in? It's simple to do. Send it out with a self-addressed, stamped envelope so you'll get it back. Make their job easy for them and easy for you. Is that the only tool you should use to recruit somebody? Certainly not. It just gives you more information. And it helps you to determine what the basic knowledge the coach has in relation to what you need.

Make Sure a Prospect Is Eligible for Your School Before You Invest Your Time In Recruiting Him or Her

I once worked for a coach who would not make a home visit until we physically had a transcript in our hands. Imagine yourself as an assistant to a recruiter, waiting to set up home visits until you had a transcript in your hand. This coach was very successful, but he would not make a home visit until we had seen the player's transcript. After three years of recruiting, I began to see that as a good idea.

At first, when I was just starting out, I thought that was kind of silly because it was a lot of work. But you can save yourself a lot of wasted time by determining at the very beginning whether the player can get into your school.

What's the role of the coach in this? You can call the guidance counselor. Oftentimes you'll receive a transcript, sometimes you won't. The coach can be very effective as the source to get this to you quickly. With today's technology you ought to be able to obtain a transcript in a day.

Another thing you can do when recruiting is to invite the coach to attend the initial home visit. What you're trying to do in the home visit is to create a visual association. You want the athlete and the coach to associate you with a mental picture of what you're trying to sell. Again, because of the time limitations in which you have to recruit, you have to create a good first impression. The home visit is a great chance to make a good first impression.

I've competed against recruiters who never bothered inviting the coach to the home visit, because they evidently didn't think it was important. Sometimes it's not important. I guess you would need to know ahead of time whether the coach is involved in the decision. But I always felt it was important, even if the coach isn't involved, to invite him or her. I feel it is important to know what relationship the coach has with the family, and I can usually tell at the home visit.

Use the Coach's Resources

The coach has resources. You can obtain transcripts, standardized scores, and SAT scores from the coach once the player has taken the tests. You can get game films as well.

> "Remember that the coach has his or her own 'hidden agenda' when it comes to players."

The coach can play a big part in making sure you have the films you need and want. It's especially important if other coaches want the films. The coach sends them to one coach and that coach is supposed to send them to you. You may not receive them, so you have to make sure that the coach knows you still need them. Sometimes I would try to do this before we even arranged a home visit. If you know the juniors you are going to be recruiting, get those game films the summer ahead of time.

I always felt that it was important to view films showing different offenses and defenses, so you're seeing different skills of the athlete in different situations. I always like to see a close game; for example, a pressure game against their number one rival.

I want to see how a player reacts in high-pressure situations. I don't want to see them play the first game of the year or an exhibition game that doesn't play a part in their league or their conference. Also, I want to see their worst games, not their best game. Most coaches will send you a film of the player's best game. We all look good on our best day, don't we? I always want to see their worst game and be able to answer the question, "Are they still good enough?" If they are, from an ability standpoint, those are recruits you want to focus on.

With a trained eye, you get a pretty good feel for ability. Even when they're playing well on a film, if it's against a poor team, there's not a lot of pressure. Psychologically, they don't have the pressure to perform that well.

In reviewing the selection process, again we're trying to determine if a player fits your needs. Is this what you want? How do they fit into your program? As a recruiter, you need to have a good balance of seniors, juniors, sophomores, and freshmen. From a position standpoint, you need talent at cross positions.

A program's style of play can also influence your selection. Do you recruit players from programs that are similar to your system? If so, then you have a great opportunity to develop a relationship with coaches who play the style that you play. That way you don't have to spend a lot of time educating them about your system. You can focus on other things. Plus the transition for those players is easier.

Seek Out the Coach's Opinion

I believe it is important that you ask the coach, "How do you see your athlete fitting into my system as a recruit?" Ask them to tell you. Can the player run your system? If so, ask where the coach sees the recruit fitting in as far as playing ability. Again, you're trying to gain information. Does the coach really know your system and what's best for his athlete?

> **"The high school coach can be your biggest asset in recruiting a player."**

Finally, there is the selling process. In my estimate, this is where the majority of your time is spent. It's a never ending process. You sell your program based on the athlete that you recruit. In our particular study of written and personal contacts with coaches, parents ranked high across all three divisions.

If you think about the number of phone contacts you can have, the number of personal contacts is limited. But you can still write as many letters to the coach as you want, can't you?

So what does that mean as far as the relationship you have with coaches? You never stop cultivating that. Whether the coach has a buffer role or an active role, you always keep in mind that you need to cultivate that relationship.

The Importance of Record Keeping

Keep a file for each athlete, whether on paper or on computer. Record each written or phone contact. Each time you talk to the coach, make a note of the date and time of the conversation or contact, and what the conversation or contact included. For example, "Talked to Coach Thompson, June 6 regarding campus visit." Add any information that he or she might give you. I think that's important.

Record those powerful little statements that are made during a routine conversation. Record that on a separate sheet, keep it in the file or on the computer, so you have it right there where you need it.

Use the Campus Visit to Develop a Relationship with the Coach and the Player

On the campus visit, I always felt it was a great opportunity if you could have a coach visit while you were playing a game. You can show a coach your facilities and the academic opportunities your program offers. He or she can meet other faculty members, and develop an association with your school. You need to do that before their season starts; because once they begin playing, they're absorbed in coaching like you.

I think it's important to ask the coach for his or her support. I say, "Coach, we've been friends for a while. You have a good feel for our system and me as a coach. Do you feel that our school is a good place for your athlete?" And if he or she says, "I like it," reinforce that when you're with the family. You might say, "Well, you know, your coach indicated that he thinks our school might be a good place for you."

Usually the home visit needs to be made as close to the signing date as possible. If there's an early signing period in your division, such as post-season, you need to know when that is. Then, set up your home visits accordingly. Your contact with the coach should be made so that the coach is involved. I've also found that the relationship between the coach and the family is very important to know.

The Significance of Coaches

I really believe that, as future recruiters, we need to at least be aware of the significance that the coach has. I think this is more important now than ever. Something you should consider is determining how much emphasis you need to give to a particular coach, in relation to how involved they are in the athlete's decision. If the coach is involved, work at it. If the coach is not instrumental in the decision, spend your time where you feel the decision is going to be made.

Author Profile: Barry Copeland

Barry Copeland has 14 years of college recruiting experience as a head coach, recruiting coordinator and academic advisor. Currently an associate professor of physical education at Syracuse University, his other coaching stops include Central Michigan University, Northwestern State University, University of Wisconsin-Green Bay and Syracuse University.

SECRETS OF THE HIGHLY SUCCESSFUL RECRUITER

by Mike Deane

Talent neutralizes talent. At every level of basketball, or whatever sport that you're in, I believe there's something to be said for that. Talent neutralizes talent, but then what do you have? I think these are things that must be kept in mind when you're recruiting.

Look at What The Player *Can* Do

I had a number of guards score 1,000 points for me during my eight years at Siena.

Mark Brown, who scored 2,200 points for us, was a 5'9" guard, a coach's son; a minority kid, with a 900 SAT. He was about 145 pounds when I saw him at the Five-Star camp in August. I had grown up just north of New York City, and I watched his dad play.

His dad was one of those guys who was the playground legend. His dad was a 5'9" lefty who would score 45 points for fun every time he went out on the floor. His dad is now a very successful coach at Jersey City State, a Division III program in New Jersey.

So I put two and two together, and went after this kid hard because he was quick, clever, and could sneak through cracks. Everybody else just said, "the guy's just a Division II or Division III player." They felt he was either too small or too little.

I looked at what he *could* do. I think it's a big point to remember in recruiting and evaluation—don't spend too much time on worrying about what a guy *can't do*; figure out what he *can do* and what he might be able to learn.

Another important factor is the impact of a player's high school coach. That makes a difference when you're analyzing a recruit. Believe me, there are an awful lot of bad coaches out there, and I don't like to say that about our profession. But it's especially a concern in women's athletics.

The problem isn't whether women's athletics is or is not good or whether or not the players are good. The problem is that they don't receive the same quality coaching. I think, however, this is all beginning to change.

I was in a college coach's office the other day and they were recruiting a high school player for their program. The college coach called the high school coach and the high school coach told him, "Well, we really don't know what to do [to help our player decide]. So I just told her to watch TV and she'll figure out what team she wants to play for." That's sometimes the situation you're facing in recruiting — where you have to reach the player directly instead of working with the high school coach.

The Impact of Scouting Services on Recruiting

I think all too often we get caught up in scouting services. You don't recruit your team. You recruit to these scouting services.

How many people in your sport subscribe to scouting services? Doesn't everybody, so you get names of players? I don't know what it's like in other sports, but in basketball those things aren't worth crap, except for the names.

> **"You do what you have to with what you have."**

Have you ever seen the guys that run these scouting services? They've never played. And these are the guys that are shaping public opinion in regard to recruiting. If I lined up all the guys who have scouting services or ever did, and I asked how many had ever coached, there would be not one. None. They don't know a damn thing about the game of basketball. They know less about recruiting. Yet they have an opinion on every kid in America.

The only positive aspect of these services is through some of the camps they sponsor. They give us the opportunity to see a lot of prospects in one place when we wouldn't be able to otherwise.

We have to figure out where the kids are. We have to use more of a network than scouting services offer. Because the scouting services really don't know much about recruits.

Unfortunately, we're all forced to subscribe to scouting services, but we don't have to believe what they say. We have to use them as a vehicle. But we should also understand where the scouts are coming from and who's delivering the names to them that we eventually receive.

Your Team's Image

What you need to do is figure out what you want. What kind of team to do you want? What kind of image do you want for your program? You can't recruit against your image, and once that image is established it is extremely difficult to reshape. Define what image you want for your program. Then keep in mind that recruiting and coaching are not separate entities. They're intertwined into a larger concept — the image of your program. I think that's what recruits your players. I think it's also your reputation as a coach and the type of coach you are. That's how you recruit.

Take a look, for example, at Kevin O'Neill. He has an image as an excellent recruiter but everybody says he is suspect as a bench coach. It is difficult if your team can't shoot and they're not particularly great academically. There's a correlation between academic ability and the flexibility that you have as a coach and the adjustments that you can make and the number and the complexity of those adjustments. So now, you evaluate what you have. You do what you have to with what you have. We have to sell what we've got.

An example is what Dick Bennett does at Wisconsin. He figured out how he was going to coach. He decided to use a defensive system that is difficult to teach and requires a tremendous amount of intensity. He gets kids that are just plain tough, and they work and work and work. And those are the only kinds of players he recruits. Why recruit a guy with tremendous talent who can run and jump, but who won't go to class and won't work hard? What do you do with him in a system like that? You can't use him.

Bobby Knight is the same type of guy. He gets tough little hard-nosed kids. All are the type of players who will respect his style. Do you think Bobby Knight is any easier on his guys than Jud Heathcote was, or Gene Keady or Kevin O'Neill? I think it's an "image thing" with Coach Knight. At Indiana you get 17,000 fans at a game, all screaming and loving you. They wouldn't boo at Indiana. Look at the stuff Bobby Knight gets away with. He's an icon in the profession and he doesn't have to recruit. Recruits come to him. That's why he's fishing during July. I never see him at a camp. He doesn't have to.

> **"When players start transferring out, you have an image problem, in my opinion."**

The Ethics of Recruiting

There's always the ethics of recruiting. There are times when I don't get certain players, and it doesn't matter what the reason is. There are players who say their scholarship is worth more, that rules are violated, this guy has this edge, and this guy did this. That doesn't matter. You have an image for your program, a way you want to go about things, and that's the way you're going to do them. You do the best you can with those things and then coach the hell out of the kids when you get them. That's my philosophy.

Why Do Prospects Choose You, Anyway?

I think it's important to analyze what's most important in a prospect's decision. Analyze what is most important in *his decision*. Then analyze your ability to match his needs and his ability to match your needs. I can't emphasize that enough. If we have two centers and there's a third center out there and he's perfect for Marquette — he has the right grades — it's a perfect situation. This is the guy you'd like to have, but you already have two centers. One center is a sophomore and the other is a freshman. There's no sense bringing this kid in because now you'd have three players at the same position.

In this situation, you wouldn't have enough playing time for all three centers. Somebody will be unhappy. Somebody's parents will be unhappy. You have problems. You end up with an image problem because one of the three will probably transfer.

In my opinion, when players start transferring from your program, you have an image problem. When players fail out, you have an image problem. When you start going after junior college players and you start taking transfers, you've got an image problem. It doesn't mean I'd never take a junior college player or I'd never take a transfer. Or even that I'd never have a kid transfer from my program. But I think it's a bad idea to make any of those things a habit. I have in my mind the image of the program that I want.

Do you know what is the biggest mistake that recruiters make? Not making their move quickly enough. You must be able to evaluate quickly whether you can sign a player or not. Second place in the recruiting game is no good. You've got to know when to hold 'em and know when to fold 'em – just like the gambler.

Sometimes I'd go watch a player and come back and say, "That guy was lousy. How could we recruit him?" Sometimes it is just as important to know who not to recruit as it is who *to* recruit. So if you go on a trip and evaluate a prospect, you're never wasting time if you get film on a kid.

Get the Films

As for films, what you often receive are self-made highlight films. Don't you love those things? It's a five-minute clip. The player looks like Michael Jordan on the film. Does everything right. Dunking. Making an assist. He's defending well. He hits every three-pointer he shoots. And I call up and I say, "Could you just send me a game film?" They send the game film and the prospect can't play at all. He has about five good excerpts every game. He's not a good player. I think you want to stay away from recruiting solely based on highlight films.

I think viewing film is a very difficult way to recruit. It's like the scouting services. All they give you is an indication. You need to have a hands-on perspective and see a player in person. I've never recruited a prospect I haven't seen myself, in person. Never.

Understand this. Every player who you sign is going to shape the round of recruits. Every player that you recruit to-

Hoop Dream Drama

One of my former players, William Gates, had quite a bit of publicity because of his participation in the film "Hoop Dreams." What a gigantic distraction, every place we went. He handled it well, and never let it become a distraction for the team.

William is married. His baby daughter is seven years old now. He was married in high school, if you watched the movie, "Hoop Dreams." So in the fall, we had to send a manager to go pick her up at day care if he's going to work out. So we do that. Will had taken the year off from school, from basketball because he was struggling a little bit in school. He's married and it's hard to handle basketball. So he took a year off, and did not play.

Later, he came back to me and said, "Listen, I think I've got it in perspective." After that, he did a great job with school. He put things back in order and said he'd like to play again. I said sure. We sat down and talked and we worked out all these things because I admired the fact that he'd held his family together.

His wife was pregnant again during the 1995 season. We were playing the NIT semi-finals and we beat Penn State. The next morning we went to work out and at 10:00 I said, "Where's Will?" They said he was back in Milwaukee. I asked why. His wife was in the hospital, having the baby. So they had the second baby, a very healthy baby boy.

That same day, Will was back, because he flew in at 4:30. He suited up and played in the championship game. We had some strange stuff going on. But that particular situation was very positive. I was happy for him. He was passing out chocolate cigars. I said, "Not before the game, Will, and don't eat these things, guys."

It was an interesting situation. I don't know what makes guys do what they do. But in William's case, I was so pleased that he had handled things so well. He's just a terrific kid. He came from a very modest background.

He has been in some very tough situations. He's going to, I think, be very successful in life. So there are flip sides to everything.

day will help recruit the next generation of players. The image that you are creating through your program has a significant impact on recruiting.

You make your home visit. You have an impact on parents during the home visit. Sometimes you have an impact on the kids. But the campus visit is what is going to determine whether a kid signs or not and — more often than not — his relationship with and how he feels about your current players will make the difference.

What Determines Who You Recruit?

> **"From the very beginning, determine what direction your program is going."**

The people that you bring in to your program are going to determine what kind of people you sign. Consider Jerry Tarkanian. Now if a kid in California scores 1200 on his SATs and is a very good point guard, will he go to Stanford or will he choose Fresno State? He's going to go to Stanford because the match is better and those are the kind of kids that he will be more comfortable with. That's not to imply that Fresno State isn't as good as Stanford.

It is important to determine in what direction you're going to shape your program, because it's very difficult to reshape it. The image has an impact not only in regard to where you want your program to go, but it also shapes parents' opinions.

You can't enter a recruit's home without the parents having a preconceived notion about what your program is all about. They already have an idea about you. They've already talked to coaches.

I don't know what it's like for all sports, but in basketball when you call up a prospect and if you're the tenth school to show an interest in that kid, you aren't going to sign that player. There are too many schools going in and that kid doesn't know what he wants to do. If you're the tenth school, 25 percent of the time you're going to get canceled by that time.

As you all know, those home visits take anywhere from one to two hours. The idea of a recruiting visit sounds great in August, but all of a sudden the recruit starts to pare his choices down. They say, "Hey, I'm tired of these phone calls. These home visits are a pain in the butt."

Sometimes a prospect will say that he has always wanted to attend this or that college for this or that reason. It's difficult to change that image in two hours. If you have an image as a junior college recruiter, it's tough to change your image from that.

I'm always concerned about our team. Our team leads the nation in goatees, earrings and tattoos. I don't like that image for my program. I don't think it's fair. I don't think it's what Marquette University is all about. We won't allow the players to have earrings around basketball. They can have them on campus, I don't give a damn about that. I can't control their lives. We're also going with the "T-shirt rule" to cover up tattoos.

I think the image of your program is important. And I've been trying to sell that throughout the year. I think the guys did a good job of handling themselves, William Gates in particular (see "Hoop Dream Drama," on page five).

Rules, Regulations, and Recruiting

How do you utilize your staff when there are so many restrictions on recruiters? You are allowed one call a week to a potential recruit. I apologize to all the people who aren't in basketball, but the football and basketball people put that rule on you. It's a terrible rule.

How are you supposed to get to know a kid anymore? You can see him twice during the season. You can only talk to him once a week. You can have just three visits with him.

How can you tell if a prospect fits into your program? Does he meet your needs? It's tough. It becomes a tough gamble for coaches and players. You have to rely on your players during the visits.

Usually we have two recruiter lists. One's about 250 people long. At Marquette, we do the same thing everybody else does. We're organized from day one. We mail out letters in January. It really comes down to the top 25 or 30 players on our list. I call a prospect the first three times. Then Bo Ellis, an assistant coach and former player, calls.

Ellis starts to sell Marquette. The educational opportunities. The tradition and all those things that are integral components of the Marquette experience. He can sell Marquette because he lived it. So he makes the fourth call. Then the fifth call is made by an assistant of mine who worked with me at Siena College. He was in my wedding,

> **"You need to sell yourself and your program."**

I was in his. He was my first captain. He gets on the phone and starts to sell me.

Then I get back on the phone and make the move for the home visit. Utilize your staff. You need to know what their strengths and weaknesses are. Figure out what you have. But you must have somebody that is going to sell you and the school. My staff needs to be able to repeat what I say to a recruit on the first three calls, but in a different way.

Recruiter, Know Thyself

I think it's important to know yourself. Match yourself. Look carefully at a kid you're evaluating. Make sure they're the kind of people you want to be around and think you can coach. How far are you willing to go? Because not every kid is a great player.

I think John Thompson made a mistake in the Olympics. He didn't recruit a team. He recruited the best athletes at each position. He figured he could defend against the other teams in Europe, if his team was number one. He lost and came in second. He lost to the Russians in the championship game. I think you need to recruit a team. However, I don't think you need all "starters." I don't think you need to sign three top 100 prospects every single year.

I think you need to sign a starter a year and some players that are going to fit into your program, respect your program, sell your program, and fit into your team concept. These are guys who are going to play 12 minutes a game and play their butts off. I think that is sometimes overlooked. I think you try to find the best players that you can.

> "I don't think you need to sign three of the top 100 prospects out there every single year."

But understand my point. Recruit to the image that you want. I believe there's a positive correlation between family, academic motivation and coachability

I'm not saying a player can't be poorly prepared for the experience as long as he is academically motivated, because we all have all these resources to help our players. We all have full-time advisors, academic people that can get a kid through college. I feel a player should go to every class and try their best. They need to at least make an effort.

Attitude Is As Important As Athletics

In my program, I want guys who are coachable. There's a point where I draw the line. I don't want a player who doesn't want to go to class. I don't want somebody who isn't going to show up in study hall. I don't want any of these little problems that are going to be distractions. So I try and figure the kids out. If you're going to accept some of those distractions and work with those kids and figure, Hey, I need the talent right now, then you can make that concession.

I think the most important thing is playing time. It's simple — if you have a playing opportunity, then you're going to get a kid. If not, then you're wasting your time.

If you already have three small forwards and you're recruiting another small forward, you're not going to get that kid. Why? Because the kid is going to figure it out. He'll go where he'll play. So playing time is a big factor in recruiting.

Geography is a gigantic factor. I can't go to Mississippi and recruit a guy unless he has a grandma who lives in Milwaukee or unless no one else is recruiting him. The strength of the program is a factor. The highest level will obtain the players. So find out who you can get and work like hell to sign those kids.

There was a player who I signed that nobody seemed to be recruiting. He was the leading scorer in the state of Indiana. He was also a quarterback. He was a tough kid. We ended up signing him with our last scholarship. He scored 1400 points during his college career.

He scored 42 against Purdue during one game. Purdue wouldn't even recruit him. They said he was too slow. He scored 44 points during his junior year against them — at Purdue. Which, as far as I'm concerned, is not the easiest place in the world to play.

If you're the highest program you have a good shot at a player. Next, you need to look at all the little things. You have to go through the high school coach. I'll be honest with you, I'm not particularly good at kissing up to some of those guys.

Academics and Its Relationship to Athletics

In my opinion, the parents are also very important if you're selling an academic-oriented institution. I like the situation where you go in and the kid scored 1400 on the SAT and his mom says, "Well, tell me about education." It has been my experience that the kid is usually more interested whether he'll have a chance at the NBA or how much he's going to be on television.

> **"Parents are very important in selling an academic-oriented institution."**

You really have to show the academics if you're from a high academic institution. If you don't, then you show the quality of your program. But you figure on how to take everything and make it positive so that you come out looking good. If you don't, you're not going to get a kid, especially if you don't impress the parents.

The league your team is in, the attendance at your games, graduation rate and job prospects are important. Every time I go on a home visit, I tell the prospect the other eight players who we're making home visits with. Their numbers, their addresses, their coaches. I tell them to call those eight guys. Not many coaches do this because they don't want you to know who else they're recruiting. I say I'm recruiting these eight guys. For three positions, I have three scholarships. I'd take all eight of these kids.

What we're looking for at Marquette are players good enough to receive a scholarship in our program. And I tell them that that's why we're at their house. They say, "Well, are you offering me a scholarship?" I tell them that it's much too early for us to determine that. I say that the reason I can't tell them is that because every time I make an official visit it's a two-way street. We evaluate him and he evaluates us. The key is, we still haven't evaluated him with just this one official visit. Now if I told his mom that we were going to offer him a scholarship ahead of time, I'd be in trouble. Don't make promises you can't keep. You never tell a kid he's going to start. What if he doesn't?

Summer Employment and Your Team

What about summer jobs? I make a list of every summer job our kids have, what they do, how much they made. Then I look at why this kid didn't make a lot of money. It's because he's from Canada, he doesn't have a green card, so he has to work on campus. He gets campus rate for his work. That's all we can do.

Another player made a lot of money because he was willing to work hard and get dirty and sweaty and work construction. Another guy didn't want to do that, so he made $7 an hour. Still another player only worked part-time because of summer school. But I make a record of every guy and his job so that they know what kinds of jobs are available. Then the parents don't start asking, Well, what can you do for my son, what's the alumni going to do for him? When they start asking that, I'm out of there anyway.

Building Rapport

The relationship between a head coach and his assistants is important, but the relationship with the players is much more important. The support service people need to be available to that kid. The assistant has to sell the kid on the program – and he has to do it in 15 minutes. Then he's the guy who is going to get him through school, if he's a marginal kid. If he's a good kid — and I say this all the time, too — who have A's and B's coming into college? We can arrange for tutors for that, to get the A, and what's wrong with that? You work that to your advantage.

> "The relationship you have with your players is very important."

What are we selling? At Marquette, we try to sell the quality and depth of our program, including the tradition, TV exposure, media attention, and facilities. And we have the worst facility in the world. Our women played there and they're now moving downtown to the Mecca. We play at the Bradley Center. So when a prospect walks onto the campus and he sees the old gym, he says, "You guys practice here?" I say, "Yeah, it's pretty good. It was good enough for Bo Ellis and Doc Rivers. It's going to be good enough for you, too. We actually play our games downtown." So you figure out how to take a negative like that and turn it into a positive.

Selling The Program

We sell our program by citing the attendance and league we are in, and the success of your former players. Every home that I walk in, I show the parents all of the kids that played four years for me, what their degree was in, and what they're currently doing. I want the parents to have an idea of what Marquette can do for their child. It's not necessary that everybody graduates, because I don't think parents expect that everyone will.

I sell a Jesuit education. I sell the campus life. Marquette is in the middle of the city. It's an ugly place, but we figure out how to make it a positive. There's no football, so basketball is king. That's how you sell that. And if football's real big, you figure out how to make that work.

What Are You Looking For In A Recruit?

We're after character. We're after talent. Of course we want athletic-oriented kids, but we need players to have an academic desire at Marquette or they won't make it. I want players with good social skills. I want a guy who is, at the very least, hungry to take advantage of his opportunity.

We look for academic preparation. Family situation. Talent level. His attitude and toughness are a key against our level of competition. We're playing the likes of Cincinnati, Memphis and Louisville. The players have to be tough.

A player has to have potential. There's an awful lot of guys who aren't quite there. There are kids who never played in high school, but who have potential. You can help guys get bigger. Remember what they *can* do, not what they *can't* do.

Personality is important. I want an image on campus that not every kid is a communications major. We need players who are academically motivated so that our program has a better fit into the entire campus. That doesn't mean I won't take some marginal students and kids who want to major in communications. I like the idea of three players coming in with 1100 SATs and each of them takes a different direction.

> **"I want to recruit a guy who is hungry to take advantage of his opportunity."**

Evalute Your Program

You need to figure what your program's weaknesses are and what your strengths are. I believe that you should use enough open-ended questions when talking to a prospect on the phone. I'm not very good at that. I tend to talk at him instead of with him.

I think the ability to get recruits to open up so you can learn more about *them* is a very important technique that should be developed in recruiting.

Honesty, Greed, and Recruiting Today

I don't like go-betweens when I recruit. A red flag goes up when I'm not dealing directly with the high school coach or parent. That usually means they want more than room and board, books, fees and tuition. I won't pursue a recruit beyond a certain point. I'm quick to get out — maybe too quick sometimes — to stop talking to some potential recruits if I think something is going on.

I think my strength is that I'm very honest in recruiting. I don't use negative recruiting. I don't spend time insulting other coaches or their programs. I may point out differences and make comparisons, but I won't run a coach's reputation into the ground.

I have a positive attitude with the parents. I always deal with high school coaches so you can come back and you can work with them again. If you're positive with high school coaches, you can come back again because you're looked at favorably.

What Do I Think Is Important?

Our program strengths, I think, are that I have the ability to laugh at myself. I also utilize my assistants well. You need a supporting president, you need key faculty people who are going to help sell your school. Your players are key and your budget is critical. I have to be able to practice until 5:00 and then fly to Memphis to see a kid if I want to. At this level, that's what you have to be able to do. We have enough money to do that.

Recruiting in Division II

In Division II, here's what you need. Most importantly, you need friends who coach Division I and make a lot of recruiting mistakes. That's what you need. Don't laugh.

You also need to talk to junior college coaches as well as high school coaches. The admissions personnel at your school are also critical. You have to be able to get marginal kids in, but you have to have a proven track record first so that you can be successful with them.

> "The most important thing is to have the support of the school's administrators."

You also need an academic vice president who is going to help when your player has nine credits to go, it's his fourth year and you don't have enough money in your scholarship pool to pay for the fifth year like we do at Division I. If he needs three independent study credits, or we need to waive one requirement, or we need to do some other things for this player to get his degree, you need to be able to count on help from the admissions and administration personnel.

Recruiting In Division III

In Division III, financial aid people are a lot more important than admissions personnel. They're especially helpful with the minority assistance programs. Financial aid in Division III is *critical*.

In Division III recruiting, a car is really your only asset, because usually you don't have a budget that's worth a darn. Let me repeat – *the car is critical* – and I'll tell you why.

One time, I was recruiting Phillip Randall in Queens, New York, driving a state-issued car. I came out of Phil's house after having spent about three hours there. Then I drove off and my car broke down, right on the corner of Union and Hall Streets in Queens. I went back up to Phil's house and called the school.

They told me to get the car towed and go to a Holiday Inn. In Queens, there's not a Holiday Inn on every corner. I told them I had 20 dollars in my pocket, because they were only paying me $9,000 a year. I also had a New York State credit card.

I asked them, What do you want me to do? They said, Well, get the car towed and leave it at the gas station. That night, I slept at Phil Randall's house.

The good news is, Phil came and played for me, even after all that. He was a JC All-American. So maybe it was a good move. There might be something in that. But your car can't break down on you. You have to have a darn good car in Division III, or else.

You also need wealthy families because you have to have kids who can pay their own way for school. And then you have to recruit undersized postmen. In Division III, that's a key. I was successful with a lot of Division III postmen.

The Resources Are Out There...If You're Looking for Them

I just gave away all the secrets that I know about recruiting. The best thing about this is that I had to go back and really take a hard look at what we do in recruiting and I think it helped me.

The fact that you are interested in what I have to say obviously indicates that you want to be good at recruiting. There certainly are a number of people out there who are going to help you. Good luck.

Author Profile: Mike Deane

Mike Deane is the head men's basketball coach at Marquette University. Mike has 23 years of college recruiting experience, including 17 years on the Division I level. He has won numerous coaching awards and has taken all of his Division I teams to the NCAA tournament. Mike's other coaching stops include Dehli A & T Junior College, Oswego State, Pottsdam State, Plattsburgh State, Michigan State and Siena College.

GUIDELINES FOR THE FIRST-YEAR RECRUITER

by Rod Delmonico

Back in 1983, when I began coaching at Florida State, I had been a graduate assistant for two years at Clemson. Every so often at Clemson, the head coach would call me in and say, "Rod, I have a player down in Columbia, S.C. I want you to go and take a look at and then come back and tell me if he can play. Don't talk to him; just go look."

So I would visit the school and come back with my report: "Well, I think he's a pretty good player." The coach would ask me, "How much (scholarship) money would you offer him?" And I would tell him.

I am fortunate, because the one thing I think I have is the ability to evaluate talent. I think it's my strength. I can see a player, evaluate him and then have a pretty good idea of what that player is able to do. That's an important part of recruiting.

I landed the job at Florida State and went down there as a third assistant. The second assistant quit right in the middle of July. He was the recruiter. He went on the road, handled the paperwork, and set up everything. Now I was stuck with recruiting. I'd never made phone calls or anything like that. I had no idea what to do. I literally just taught myself.

The only thing I ever read about recruiting was an article back in the 80s in *Sports Illustrated* about how Jim Valvano recruited a player. It talked about his assistants and a technique they used to recruit players. They use a room they spent about $30,000 on — where the recruit sits in a special chair and smoke comes up and the chair rotates and he sees the national championship rings, and the picture of winning it all. To top it off, they'd have his jersey on the wall. That was the only thing I ever read about recruiting. I learned more by word of mouth, by talking to people.

In baseball, during the 1970s and early 1980s, the way we recruited was to fly one or two prospects in. That's all we could afford with our budget. We didn't have the budget that football or basketball teams have, allowing us to bring in 20-25 guys for visits and spending the money to see them three or four times.

We had to spend a lot of time on the phone. What happened back then was you would pick up the phone and find a player who was either drafted in the third or fourth round, or you'd find a prospect who was an all-state junior college player. You'd call him up and ask, "Would you like to come to Florida State?" If he agreed, we'd tell him what kind of scholarship we could offer him. He'd say, "Great, I can't wait to get there."

In the early 80s, people started working at it. Now, another school would call him up and say, "Would you like to play?" He'd say, "No, I'm going to Florida State." The recruiter would say, "I've got $5,000 for you. We'll take care of all your tuition." All of a sudden, we started a formal recruiting process in college baseball.

Times Have Changed

> "Recruiters now need a system to be successful in putting a good team together."

In my 17 years of recruiting in baseball, it has drastically changed. We have caught up a little bit with football and basketball. We now have to have a system. We now have to use a computer. We have to spend time with our juniors as much as we do with our seniors.

One thing I've found is that recruiting is the lifeblood of your program. If you don't outwork your opponents off the field, they will beat you on the field. Another thing I've noticed is that the assistant coaches do the majority of the recruiting and spend a lot of time making phone calls and evaluating players. Assistant coaches don't get enough credit for the hard work and the time they spend out there. That's not taking anything from the head coaches. The head coaches do their part, but the assistants, I've found, do the bulk of the recruiting.

When I went to Florida State, it was easy to recruit the first couple of years, because I was with a program that was rich in tradition. I think it's easy to recruit at Notre Dame for football or Kentucky for basketball, because kids *want* to go there. I found that players around the country wanted to come to Florida State, because Florida State was in the College World Series. So when you called them up and said, "I'm from Florida State," you instantly got their ear.

The first couple years I was at Tennessee, when I called players up and said, "I'm from Tennessee," they knew of Tennessee football but had never heard of Tennessee baseball. So it's entirely different recruiting at a smaller institution or an institution that has very little tradition, versus recruiting at a name school like Florida State. It was easy to get my foot in the door. Once that was accomplished, I could get on with the recruiting process.

The Ability to Evaluate

The number one consideration in the recruiting process is **evaluation.** It's crucial that you have somebody on your staff who can evaluate talent. There are some coaches who recruit with their ears, others with their eyes, and others with their hearts. In other words, you need someone on your staff who can see a young man, in our sport, for example, go zero-for-three and not touch the baseball and be able to come back and say, "I think he's got a chance to hit for us. I think he has a chance to be a player."

I know I've been to games and have seen players hit home runs, only to come back and say, "He can't play for us; he doesn't have the *ability* to play for us." If you're dealing with basketball or football, you have a lot of game footage. Some high schools and junior colleges are now videotaping their players, so that they can give us something to help with our evaluation process. However, videotapes aren't too effective when we evaluate a pitcher, because of factors such as velocity, the mound, the field, the set-up, hand speed, whether he's a 4.4 second runner to first base, or whether he's a 3.4 second runner from the time he moves to first base to the time he steals second base.

The Importance of Potential

The second factor to consider in recruiting is **potential**. You have to be able to evaluate, or project, a player to see how far he can go. I really believe recruiting, when we put together our team, is very much like painting a picture. We sit down every year and figure out what we need to make this team a little bit better. Our goal is to create a team that can get us to the College World Series.

> "It isn't enough to look at what is. You also need to consider what will be."

I believe assistant coaches need to have the same "burning desire" the head coach has. The coaching staff has to be a family. If you don't share the same goals, you're missing out. I love to compete off the field – winning by signing a great player is just as exciting as winning on the field. Assistant coaches need to have that same desire to succeed. That "burning desire" will keep you up late at night; it'll give you the edge.

Does He Have Heart?

The last key is the **heart**. Can you evaluate with your heart? Do you have a sixth sense or a gut feeling about whether or not this is the kid you want? I had an athlete who played second base for us. His name was Ed Lewis. He was an individual who in high school was just a pretty good player. I had a feeling that he was going to work hard enough to one day to develop into a good player. He was a .220 hitter his first two years. Believe me, I had some doubts about whether or not my gut feeling was right. But then he hit over .400 in SEC play in 30 games, and he hit around .330 for us. He was really the difference in our team getting to the College World Series. He was a good solid high school player, and I thought he had character and a lot of heart. I had a gut feeling that this recruit was the kind of player who would fit into our program.

We believe our team is a family and we stress that with everyone, from the coaching staff right down. We had a great player in Tennessee that we did not recruit one year. I had players from our team who grew up in his hometown who told me, "Coach, he doesn't fit in here. He'll stick out. He's not part of the family. He's got a personal agenda that won't fit into our program. He's not the type of player that we want." So we didn't recruit him. Not only do we recruit, but we also have our players recruit for us.

The next thing we try to do in evaluation is to determine what type of character a recruit has. Can this player advance to the next level for us? We also try to work very hard to recruit juniors and underclassmen. We set up a mailing system with two letters – one saying, "You've been recommended" and another stating, "We appreciate your interest."

We receive over 100 letters a month from players who write in to say they want to come to play for Tennessee. We write every one of those guys back, using a form letter that includes information about our program plus a questionnaire. I personally sign every one of those letters. We try to make it as personal as we can.

Develop a Recruiting System

One of the easiest things I did (when I didn't have a computer back in '83) was to come up with a top file A and a top file B. Our top file A was used when we went on the road; if we had our top file with us, we had all the information needed to call our recruits. I used a folder and inside I put the questionnaire and every letter that we had sent a recruit. On the inside cover I've got 4-5 sheets of paper stapled, so I can jot notes every time I talk to the recruit.

Other recruiters probably have computers to store information, but what I did was put all the information together in a file – things about mom and dad, background items, his coaches, everything on the questionnaire.

So every time we call on the recruit, I put a little note in the file. We have two assistant coaches, so every time we make a call to a young man, we write down anything that will help us in the recruiting process. As we're recruiting, we record all sorts of information for reference. If I go in and say, "Larry, I want you to call Auggie tonight," he opens the folder and he can quickly read down through the little messages or memos there on each conversation. He knows the last time we talked to him. He can pick up the phone and say, "I understand you went three for four last week and had the game winning hit; what happened this week?" The recruit might say, "I've eliminated Miami; it's between you and Texas." All this goes in the file.

Once we have set up our top files, we take all the information from every top file that we have on each player and we put it all on a sheet of paper. We have a depth chart on the top so that we have the top shortstops we're recruiting, the second basemen, the first basemen, left fielder, center fielder, right fielder, whatever. Then you open it up and we've broken it up into pitchers, catchers, infielders,

> **"Information is the key to success in recruiting. The more you know, the better."**

outfielders. Next to every player's name, I have his mom and dad's name, his high school coach's name, his mom's phone number, his dad's phone number, and numbers where the recruit can be reached.

Recruiting Isn't A One-Time Thing

The other thing we try to do is to spend some time writing notes from on the road or making phone calls. The biggest thing that I have found that has changed in the last 10 years is the lazy coach – the coach who does nothing. He starts recruiting in December for basketball, for football he starts recruiting in June, for baseball for the next season – the lazy coach just caught up with the rest of us that really work. It used to be that you could write to juniors as well as seniors

Other things have changed. When we were in the College World Series in 1986-'87, I took my top file into the dugout when I was with Florida State and we'd have 15 minutes before the game. I'd call our top kids right from the dugout. I'd say, "I'm right here in Omaha; we're getting ready to play in a few minutes. Catch us on the tube." You can't do that anymore. The only thing we can do now is call from the hotel and say, "Catch us tonight; we're playing on ESPN." But I think that little extra touch helps you along the way.

The system that we put together, with our top file and our mailing system, prepares us to go after recruits. We've got our top kids, the 35 kids we're going to recruit. The second part is our B file. Our B file includes all the junior college players, the second line player or third line player. We spend a lot of time recruiting those prospects. We have a fall signing period in November and then the April signing period. Fall is when we do the bulk of our recruiting and pick up our eight to ten guys. In April we'll pick up maybe one or two players. We have to have a plan B, which I would compare to basketball and football in that if you sign a player and all of a sudden he's not academically eligible.

We have a "follow file." In that file are great juniors, rising sophomores, kids in camp. There might be 16 or 17 kids. We just want to follow their progress and see how they're doing in our community. But more important are the second line players — the players who have been passed over but all of a sudden start to click. One might be a great left-handed pitcher who wins eight games; maybe he only throws 83-84 miles per hour, but he knows how to pitch.

We spend a lot of time recruiting those types of players. We try to write our players and use a series of letters that we send out not only to coaches, but the first time that we write a player as a junior or as a senior. Because of regulations, you're limited to the amount of time that you can write a sophomore or junior or what you can say to them. But we have a series of letters that we send out to a junior coach and a junior player, as well as a senior. For example, we'll send 15 letters out, one or two every month. We'll send a letter out to the coach. For instance, if we have a top player in Virginia, we'll send a letter to his folks, talking about his play, saying we'd like to keep in touch with him. Then we'll follow up with a phone call. Then we'll come back and send a letter saying we wish him good luck in the season and hope things are going well. We'll do the same thing with the parents. We'll write the parents individually. Then we'll write the player. We try to touch all avenues. We try to build good rapport with the coaches and spend a lot of time with them. I have found in recruiting in our sport, it's important to keep in touch with the coaches. You don't know who's going to make the difference in a young man's decision or be an influence. Is it going to be the mom, dad, an uncle, high school coach, a junior college coach, or a friend of the family? Who's the guy who's going to push this kid in one direction?

> **"We've use a series of letters to keep in touch with prospects and their coaches."**

With the phone call system, we're limited to one call a week But that one call a week limit is to the athlete. We try to touch base with the high school coach or the junior college coach more often.

I think letters are probably one of the easiest ways to reach the player and not put demand on him. You get to a point when you run out of things to talk about on the phone. I have found it's much easier to put something in the mail to him, so the young man can read it and pick it up and follow that with one phone call. Also, fill the mailbox with information that's going to help. The article that I read back in the early 1980s on Valvano's program said that letter writing was very big. So we made up a card that has a picture of our stadium on it; we spend a lot of time writing on these postcards — just handwritten messages, little notes. If we see that a player went three for four or had the game winning hit, we pick up a postcard and send a message to him.

When we went to Vegas or California or if we were at the Superdome in Seattle, I'd purchase 35 postcards and jot down a little note saying, "We're playing here," or whatever, and pop the card in the mail to the prospects.

The Relationship Between Coaches and College Recruiters

Contacting the high school coach or the junior college coach really makes a difference for us. It is important to build a rapport with the coach. If you think about it, the player's high school coach or his junior college coach is really the guy that he's close to. He spends a lot of time with him. Very seldom does he spend as much time with his mom and dad as he does with his high school coach.

> "Little things can mean a lot."

I'm always with my guys and I think I've got their ear, especially when it comes to draft situations. They ask me what I think. The key is to educate the high school coach and make sure he gets a media guide so that he knows about your program. I want to educate the high school coach to our program, our coaching staff, and what we can offer.

These are things that I think give us an edge. Whether they help us or not, they give us a little bit of an edge. I send a letter of congratulations to the top 25 coaches named in *USA Today* baseball and any coach who receives a Coach-of-the-Year award. I sign it at the bottom, congratulating them on being picked fourth in the country in the last poll. I tell them that I hope we can recruit some of their players one day and to keep us in mind if they have a great player or two.

The list comes out three or four times a year, and we do it every year. Now when you call a coach and say, "This is Rod from Tennessee," he knows you. You wrote him a letter of congratulations, and he's going to appreciate the fact that you took time out of your busy schedule to write.

Honesty Is the Best Policy

I think you have to be honest with your players, always. We don't pull any punches. I don't try to tell them what they want to hear. I'll never tell a player that they're going to start at Tennessee. I'll never tell a high school coach that his player's going to be our number one pitcher. If you're honest and you get out there and do what you're supposed to do and you're honest with the high school coach and the players, it's going to help you down the road.

I do think you need to put together a game plan. You show them what can happen if they come to your school — what can happen down the road. Give them a road map of what's going to happen. But you have to be honest with them. Don't tell them they're going to be an All American, if they have no chance of being All American. Don't tell them they're going to start for you as a freshman, if they can't start for you as a freshman. That will come back to haunt you. I see a lot of recruiters out there who tell players whatever they want to hear.

My recruits love to have the opportunity for a challenge. I don't know if they can play here, but they're going to get an opportunity. That's what we share with them. I don't know if they can be on starting rotation. I don't know if they can play second base, but we're going to give them an opportunity.

The walk-on program is important. "Walk-on" for us means we might give a recruit a book scholarship or $1,000. It's really about a young man who wants an opportunity to come into the program and work hard. We have to live and die by our walk-ons.

You never know. I've found that the player that I give 60% (of a full scholarship) or less is my best player. Most of the time 80 and 90% guys, those guys are not hungry; they don't get after it. It's the guy that I give 60% to, the next year 70%, and the next year I give him 80%. When he's a senior, I put him on 90-95%. Those are my best players. They're hungry. That's what I look for. The young man who loves to play the game and has a passion for baseball and wants to compete. That's the kid that you win a championship with. Those are guys that are not the most talented, but they outwork everybody on the staff.

The Relationship Between Players and Recruiters

If you look at our team, you'll see I'm blessed. God has blessed me to be able to recruit and coach. This is a great profession, being a coach. I am so fortunate to be able to go out there and work with these guys. They are super individuals. And you know what, great players recruit great players.

> **"Your players can be the difference between a prospect signing with you or not signing."**

When we bring our players in the fall, I tell them, "There are two things I want you to do for our recruiting. One is to sell our program. Second, if we bring in a problem player, you have to live with him for three years. I don't have to room with him. I don't have to eat with him. I have to deal with him on the field for three or four hours, six or seven days a week. You're with him 24 hours a day. You have to go to the football game with him. This is your team. Not *my* team. It's *your* team. *Our* team. You need to help me in recruiting."

The other thing is that when we bring in a player, I say, "We have to know if he'll fit in our family. Does he have character? Is he the right kind of player? When he goes out, does he have class?" You'll know that in two days. It's amazing. One fall we had two players in, one from Florida and one from Tennessee. We met up in our press box, overlooking the field. Afterwards I asked our catcher, who was playing third base that night, "How did you like so and so?" He said, "He's a great guy." I asked him what he thought of the other prospect, one of the top players in Tennessee. He said to me, "That guy, no way. Don't recruit him." So I listened. We didn't offer him a scholarship.

It will kill you if you get a bad kid. You might see a guy who can slam dunk, do a 360, throw a ball 90 yards from end zone to end zone, throw 95 miles an hour. But if he's not the right kind of person for your program, he will bring your team down. Sometimes when you see our team play, you will not see the most talented team. Some years we probably have the least talent at the College World Series. The way I explain my players is, if I was in a foxhole in World War II, with 2,000 enemy soldiers coming up the hill, and I had my team in that foxhole, I'd look at them and say, "Fellas, let's go get them." With some other teams, I'd shoot myself. That's how I explain my team. They have some character. And that's the difference.

I try to build character and the mental approach. Some people talk today about the psychology of coaching. Give me a player who's got great fundamentals, someone who will do everything I tell him to do and is mentally tough. Boy, we'll win some games. But a superstar, who's off on his own personal agenda, that guy will kill your ball club. Our All Americans don't act like All Americans with our team, attitude-wise. You'd never know who was eighth pick of the Rockies.

The Relationship Between Your Players and Recruits

Your players recruit players. One thing we do when we bring in recruits for a visit is to put them with our players. We'll go to breakfast with them. I'll take them out to dinner, but then I want them to spend time with our players. Mostly, I want them to experience the family atmosphere. Players that we recruit will come to me and say, "Coach, you were right. Your guys are cool."

Seventeen of them at a time will go to a football game. A bunch of them will go to the movies at night. They'll just all meet, go to the movies, and eat popcorn. You build a sense of family in your team and you have something special. That's the key. I want the recruits to come in and feel what it's like. They tell me, "Coach, I can't believe how close your guys are. You have some great guys. I can fit in here. I feel comfortable with these guys."

In-House Visits

In the area of in-house visits, we're trying to catch up with football and basketball. You have three visits; they go in-house all three times. We're just starting to do that the last eight or nine years in college baseball. You'll see the head coach go for two visits; an assistant coach will go for one. It was very seldom in the early 80s that I ever made two visits to a house, unless the recruit was in our area.

> **"The amount of money you have determines what you do in your recruiting efforts."**

We never flew out and made two visits. But our recruiting budget has grown. You might be in a situation where you just don't have the money to be able to go out for visits.

What we did in the early stages, before we had money to go out and recruit, was to go out one or two times a year. When I was at Florida State, our head coach would make maybe two or three visits a year and that was it. I made sure the recruit knew that was the case. I'd turn a negative into a positive and let the recruit know that he was special enough for a visit. Now, we have a little more money and we try to get out as much as we can.

When we visit, we make it short and sweet. I have a little booklet that I put together especially for recruiting. It gives recruits and parents an idea of the activities on campus. We also have a highlight videotape that we show. After I leave the house, the parents know everything about Tennessee, from the academics to our athletic program to our history and objectives. The information includes charts that illustrate our goals for the program. I want to try to cover everything in two hours. When I leave, the parents have a good feeling about me and they know about our program and about our players. In our sport, most of the moms and dads do not visit. Very seldom do parents come with recruits for on-campus visits.

If you really think about the recruiting process, it's one of the hardest sells in the world. You go into a shoe store and you try on the shoes, you walk around the store, it's an easy sell. But when you have to go into a home or call parents on the phone and talk to them 20 or 30 minutes and tell them about your program, that's difficult. They know nothing about you. That's a very difficult sell, especially in two or three months. The earlier you can get started in the process of educating the parent, the better.

The Winning Edge

> "The three keys to success are facilities, winning and recruiting great players."

There are a couple of things that I believe have made our program a little better than some of the others. I think you just brainstorm. Fifteen years ago when I started at Florida State, the burning desire for me, a young assistant who had never recruited before, was try to take our program to another level in recruiting. I think you build your program in three areas: facilities, winning, and recruiting great players. Every year you have to upgrade your facilities. You have to do better on the field — win more games, win championships — and you have to recruit better players. That's something that we've tried to do every year. Facilities, winning, and recruiting great players – those are the three cornerstones of our program that will never change.

Recruiting is the lifeblood of your program. I don't care what anybody says — if you can't recruit, you can't be the greatest coach in the world. Great players make great coaches. If I ever receive any accolades as a head coach, it will be a direct result of my assistants and my players. Bad players get coaches fired. Simple as that. So if you can't recruit, you can't coach. You can be the greatest on the fundamentals of the game, but you better have the horses. They can pull you out any time. A coach can make a stupid mistake and the great players – the solid players – will pull you out.

With our small recruiting budget, I made an audio tape. I rounded up a radio announcer and said, "We're going to make a tape on one of our players." The coach was interviewed for the tape and he talked about the player being a great pitcher. Then we went to the regional and taped him starting a championship game in the regional. Then the first game of the College World Series. On the tape, we mentioned that he was there for his team all year — a big winner in the regional, he had a big win in Miami, won the series down in Miami.

During recruiting, we would take the prospects to the stadium on a Friday night. We'd turn the lights on and I'd take them in. We'd be talking and I'd say, "This is a great place to play. We have a tremendous tradition. What a beautiful place. I've always liked the night games. Isn't this a gorgeous park?" Then, boom. On the speaker would come, "And here we are in Miami. Big game between the Hurricanes and the Seminoles..." It would go on, about a six minute tape. The radio announcer would do pitch by pitch; you would hear crowd noise and the whole bit. The prospect would get goose bumps as he sat there listening to the tape. Or we'd play it on the way to the airport. Pop it

> **"Dare to be different and stand out from the pack."**

in and let them listen. "Son, this is what it's like to play here and this is what can happen to you if you come here next year." We would also send a tape to a recruit's home. The parents would be able to hear my voice and understand what was going on in our program. You can't do that anymore, but that gave us an edge.

Find a Way to Set Your Program Apart from the Crowd

Another time, we brought in a player during my second year at Tennessee. I called the Louisville Bat Company and told them I needed a bat with the name "Jason Cox" on it. I also asked for a glove with the recruit's name embroidered on it. I spent $100 on the glove and $12.50 on the bat. He walked into the locker room and I have his uniform with his name on the back — no big deal; a lot of schools do that. We had everything that we could give him legally: a helmet and his own bat and glove. It took him back. He saw his name on the back of the uniform, and then he looked down and saw the bat and glove. He said, "Coach, can I have this?" I told him, "Yeah, I'll give you that. I just need an autograph. You give me an autograph on signing day, and I'll give you that bat and glove next year. When you come in, you can have that glove to use. You can have that bat."

It really juices them up on their visit; it's amazing. When they walk in and they see their name on the back of a jersey, that just fires them up. I don't know why. They love having their name on the back of the jersey. We do that with a bat or a glove. And if you don't sign him, you send it to wherever he goes.

Recruiting and Academics

Academics is an important part of the recruiting process. I hear recruits sometimes say that other coaches didn't talk about academics. We get them in to see the school, and they meet the president. We'll also have a professor in the business department sit down and share with the recruit where we rank nationally in accounting, or whatever. If we can get them in on Friday, we have them go to class with one of our players, so he can sit there in the classroom and feel a part of what it's like to be in a classroom.

Prepare Your Players For Their Life After College

> **"The strengths of your program should be athletic <u>and</u> academic oriented."**

If you honestly don't believe that academics are important, the players will know that. If you're a coach who believes the most important thing is coming here and helping win a championship, they'll know that. I believe the most important thing that I can give my players is a diploma and prepare him academically. Three percent of our guys get to the big leagues. Most of our kids, 97%, are going to go out into the work force. Academically, if he gets a degree, he's going to be able to make several million dollars in the next 40 years. He's going to be able to provide for himself. So you better be truthful with them about academics. They need to know about the tutorial system. They need to know that if you miss class, in our program, you miss the game the next day. Our football coach won't do that; our basketball coach won't do that. Maybe it's because they have fewer games than we do. But if I catch a guy missing class, that costs a game. Academics are that important to me.

Get Involved to Get Recruits

Another key is that we are active in our community. We have done two things in our community and our state that have helped us tremendously. First, we get into our community in a camp situation. I'm not going to kid you, one of the reasons I have a camp is to make some money. Our camp draws around 1,300 kids. That's one of my goals. The other goal is to put something back into baseball.

I teach these young men the proper way to play the game of baseball. The third reason is to recruit. One of our first basemen went to a satellite camp in Chattanooga. He was a ninth grader at the time and could really swing a bat. We started working with him and brought him up to our camp. Next thing you know, he signs. He was a freshman team All American with *Baseball America*. It all started with our satellite baseball camp.

The other thing we have is a Big Orange Coaching Caravan. We put on eight of those. We get 50 to 100 coaches in a room, and for four hours on a Monday night we talk about catching, throwing, hitting, and how to run practice. We educate the coaches. If we get 50 coaches and they have 10 players on each of their teams, we have been able to reach out to 500 kids. If I do eight caravans, I can reach out to 3500 players. Not directly, but indirectly. I'm building a network of people around us who are all thinking baseball. We charge $25, but each coach gets a 40-page notebook with all of our catching, throwing, and hitting information.

The last thing we did involved a state clinic. Last year we had over 300 coaches for our third year. We had some great instructors come in, but we reached out to the entire state and our community. We're trying to educate our coaches and build a relationship in the community that will filter up. We work very hard to build a foundation of players for years to come. I want those kids growing up wanting to play at our school, wearing our uniforms. That's the key.

Passion is the Key to Recruiting Success

The only thing I can share with you is that I hope you understand that I have a passion about my sport. I have a passion to coach and I have a passion about recruiting. I love to recruit. It involves long hours, lots of phone calls, and lots of organization. But you must have passion. If you don't have that passion, you're missing out as a recruiter. If you have a passion and if you're really juiced up about recruiting and about your sport, you'll find a way to beat your opponent.

When I started in '83 I had no idea what I was doing. I learned through hard knocks to figure out what did work or didn't work. A few things prevailed: hard work, getting after it, being honest with the people you deal with, and trying to get better as a recruiter. I think if you keep those things in mind and work hard, good things will happen to you. To be a great recruiter you have got to work extremely hard. The rewards will be there on the field — and after they leave, academically, what happens to them as an individual.

Author Profile: Rod Delmonico

Rod Delmonico is the head baseball coach at the University of Tennessee. A National Region and Conference coach-of-the-year award winner, his recruiting classes have been ranked in the top ten for eight consecutive years. Other coaching stops include Gloucester County Community College, Clemson University and Florida State University.

DAVID VS. GOLIATH: COMPETING WITH CADILLAC PROGRAMS

by Bill Foster

When you've been in recruiting for a while, it's easy to get discouraged. Things don't go the way you want them to. What looked like a great group of players doesn't "click" well together. You lose a great prospect to a bigger school. You begin to wonder what's gone wrong. And then it all turns around.

You look at your "sudden" success and try to figure out what happened. What were you doing differently now when compared to just a little while ago? What did it for you? People did it. Personnel did it. Talent did it. And a coaching staff. But the talent of the players really makes the coaches look good. Analyzing where your success comes from is an important part of what we do as recruiters. There are specific things you can do to make sure that you are successful.

Know Thy "Enemy"

First, you have to identify your competition. Who are the "Cadillac" programs? I can remember my second coaching job. I was going into a high-powered high school, high-powered academically, that didn't have high-powered basketball.

I studied the schools that were very, very successful. I looked at who won the state. I surveyed how many baskets they had compared to what we had. I found out how many coaches they had, and that type of thing. The biggest thing is to identify who the programs are. Who are the best teams and why?

Now you start to break that down. Why? I think one of the things that the current NCAA rules have done is to reduce the "outworking" of people. You see that so many times in recruiting. We can outwork each other in sheer volume of hours we put in — days, evenings, and weekends. In my opinion, what you have to do now is "out think" the other recruiters. You've got to be creative. I think creativity in recruiting is more important than it's ever been before.

Creativity in ideas. Creativity in financing. Cost reduction is here and it's going to stay. We're restricted somewhat by budgets and it's important what you do with the budget you have. Do you say, "We can't do this; we can't do that." Success comes in cans. Not in can't or cannots. So creativity becomes very, very important.

Analyzing, studying, thinking, and creating are important components. Brainstorm with your staff. Get ideas wherever you can and hopefully they will give you a little bit of an advantage. Through all of this, you have to be well-informed and well aware of the rules, because they are always changing. With direct mail, and things such as that, you have to be very, very careful as far as the rules are concerned. That's essential.

Stay Positive to Be Successful

> **"You must *never* engage in negative recruiting."**

I must emphasize, right from the start, that negative recruiting is out. I think that more people, more parents, and particularly more coaches and prospects, are really concerned more about the negative aspects of recruiting. When it happens, it's a turn off. It's not a turn on. You should emphasize the positive that you have and find creative ways to let prospects know what those positives are.

Every school has positive attributes. We were recruiting a player who wanted to obtain a top-notch education. His final three choices for college were Northwestern, University of Nevada at Las Vegas, and Louisiana State University. I felt good about that. That's generally not the type of recruit we're dealing with. You have to try to determine what this person wants, what's going to hit their hot button, and who are the influential people who will be involved in the decision-making process.

Invest in Character

I think one of the toughest aspects of recruiting is finding out the character of the individual. The rules right now say that you can't see a prospect as much. You're going to have to do a lot by telephone. How many coaches, honestly, are going to tell you about this young person? Personally, I get caught in a trap. A guy calls me from overseas and says, "How good of a player is this player? What are his habits?" Our job right now, all of us, is really to check the character of the individuals that we're recruiting — for many reasons.

A four-year scholarship at Northwestern is worth about $100,000. That's expensive. And scholarships are being reduced. I'm talking from the standpoint of men's basketball right now. Our scholarships went from 15 to 14 to 13. Do we have a big financial investment in these young people? You'd better believe it. We also have another investment — graduation rates.

We hold ourselves to a different standard at this level, because the local newspaper is going to say this player left or transferred because he's unhappy, or whatever. How do you define happy? This one really gets me. I wish they'd put out a happy wand. That might be a good marketing idea, to put out a happy wand, so we could just touch somebody and they would be happy. Then they would <u>always</u> stay with your program. I think it's more popular now not to be happy at a school. You're just going to continue to see more students transferring for a lot of reasons.

That first year in school is really a delicate year. Especially for the freshmen that you have on campus, it's really a delicate time for them. They're away from home; they may be in over their heads academically. They have a ton of problems. Roommate problems. The dorm that they're in. Habits that they have, and new habits that they're picking up. Frankly, to me, it's scary.

Use Your Administrative Staff Wisely

When I was athletic director at Northwestern, one of the things that was new for me was to attend the president's staff meeting every Monday morning at 9:00. I now have a greater respect for the dean of students. She reported what happened over that past weekend at the university. Northwestern is basically a small school — 7,000 undergraduates. I can't imagine what a dean goes through at a larger school after regular weekends and the problems that come up. You've got to keep in touch with the young people and spend a lot of time with them.

The rules are going against us, as coaches. We're not allowed to have team meetings and do some things as we used to. Out of season, you're not allowed to do a lot of things. So keeping in touch has to be done on a one-to-one basis or maybe three people may come in and go over things.

Can You Measure Success?

Part of becoming a very good program is not only identifying the top people who are going to come in, but identifying a basic fit. Will this prospect fit in? Academically, socially, and basketball-wise? Because if you're going to build with character, build with good character. There are enough characters out there. Build with <u>good</u> character. I think that's important. I hope you'll keep that in mind and make good character a part of all your recruiting efforts.

> "Start local and recruit from there. Prospects who know you are good candidates."

In studying and analyzing how these programs have become successful, whether they're in your league, I think you have to start locally and work out from there. You have to have your own scouting report. Just like a coach prepares for the next opponent, you have to study recruiting so you can get better personnel to compete on an even playing field.

Your scouting report starts with a staff study. Study your own staff. Make them better. Make them aware of creativity and budget. Also, make your staff aware of the positives that you're going to accentuate. What are the strengths of your school, your program, and your area? The Chamber of Commerce can help you out here. You can do a lot with a copier. You can't do a lot right now with four-color pieces because of small budgets, but you can make copies of things. I think, at times, we overdo mail-outs.

If you look at any top prospect who signs, he or she will talk about getting a handwritten letter every day from a coach. I'll tell you what, when you hire a staff you had better hire someone who can write. I've seen some handwriting that's atrocious. There have been a couple of articles on recruiting in *Sports Illustrated* which showed copies of handwritten letters from coaches that had incorrect spelling.

So don't substitute quantity for quality. You should use quality items. I was once talking to one of our trustees in Chicago who said he was talking to our new basketball coach about the strengths of Northwestern and where we were academically. I think one of the things that we try to focus upon is enrollment. When a young person is selecting a school, so many times the size of the school is important. If it's not that important, you can sell its importance because of the fact that maybe at this particular time the recruit is attending a small high school and may not want to attend a school with a student population of 50,000. As a smaller school, you may have a better chance to have this person decide to attend your school.

Northwestern was number two in the nation, next to Harvard, in the number of graduates who were executives of Fortune 500 companies. Now I think that's a powerful statistic. Prospects don't think of this as being as important as their parents do. I think I would have done a lot better recruiting parents than I did young people for our program. We were seventh in the nation in the number of graduates listed in *Who's Who*. Something like that we try to emphasize to the prospect and the parents, and whoever is involved in the recruiting process. We want the decision-makers to be informed, whether it is an inside person or the parents or an outside person or a primary decision-maker. I think the high school coach needs to be informed, also. In so many cases, the high school coach is going to have some influence on the decision-making process.

Gather Information to Guide You

> **"Find out what your school already makes available."**

You should really look around and see what is available to attract a prospect's attention. For example, we developed a booklet — The Rules and Regulations Guide for Alumni and Friends of Northwestern University Athletes. I think the more you pick up things like this, the more ideas you will have to promote your own program.

There's a publication out there called *Basketball America*. The publication gets to young people and they read it. I would like to see some of the publications help us alert young people to what the rules are. I think for the most part they know, but the specific rules change about every six months. That's one of the tough things we have to do today — keep up with the rules. You have to study the rules.

You Can Learn How to Close the Sale

I think anytime you can get ideas on how to inform and educate prospects, it's important to do that. Anytime we can, in our recruiting, provide information that helps to educate parents and young people about the rules. It shows those individuals being recruited that we have a concern for the rules. As coaches, that's what we have to do. For the longest time, I was feeling that coaches were starting to look like the last cowboys in America. Our reputation had really started to deteriorate. Bobby Knight came up with one of the great comments of all time. It cost him any friends he had in football coaching; but he said, when the Watergate scandal was in progress, "When they get to the bottom of Watergate, they're going to find a football coach."

It could have been any kind of a coach, because what we're all trying to do is get an edge while still working within the rules, to gain an advantage. Anytime you're trying to do that from a recruiting standpoint, you've got to have information and you've got to sell that information.

> **"Use basic sales techniques in your recruiting efforts."**

Selling is repeating. You need to close the sale. I have purchased audio and video tapes on closing the sale. I've had seminars with our staff on closing the sale. I've brought people in, people who I thought were outstanding salespeople, to talk to our staff about closing the sale. Because that's part of our education. We continually have to work at educating ourselves if we're going to move up the ladder and be able to recruit the people that we need to compete at a top level.

The use of a mail-out program is important, but the more it is individualized, the more effect it will have. A little note that's handwritten is very important. I used to hand write envelopes, too. Again, the rules are now changing things to some extent.

Study the techniques for closing the sale. Your budget dictates most of what you can do in recruiting. So you have to be creative in trying to find out what you can do within your budget. Share ideas within your department. Brainstorming sessions can help you come up with ideas that may be very helpful. In sports like basketball, where one or two people can make a big difference, one good idea can make your whole career.

Success Starts with a Plan

Here's a game plan. First of all, what you're doing now has to be studied and analyzed. You can't become complacent in recruiting, mail-outs, or in your phone contacts. Stress the strengths of your program. Avoid negative recruiting. I think having a game plan and writing it down is very important for your department. And remember, personalize, don't computerize.

If you're a very small school with a very limited budget, you may have to computerize. But use your computer to do the things it does best. If you have someone on your staff who can recognize talent and who can recognize the possibility of recruiting that person, then you have a head start. Targeting is a key part of recruiting. Use your tools — computerized and human. I've had staff members whom I have asked, "Who's the best player?" And they would give me a list of 19 guys. At times we'd be recruiting 48 people. I cannot do that. So we would try to target and identify the best prospects.

One of the problems that exists is when you identify an individual who really wants to come to your school, but who is not at the talent level that is going to make you better. So targeting is a major job responsibility for an assistant coach. A coach must be able to target, to identify that one person who makes the tremendous difference for the future.

Staff teamwork is essential. If you have people working with you, you need to teach them that it's not the hours that count as much as what you put into the hours. As an administrator of a program, you need to be very, very conscious of that.

Follow your game plan. If you need extra help, consider student help, volunteer work, and work/study assistance. In your school, identify who the work/study people are, because it minimizes the drain on your budget. Freshman orientation is a great time to really target some help for your recruiting. Student help. Freshman orientation is a great place to start to look for your managers. Your managers can help with your direct mail letters among other things.

For a lot of schools, students help out by manning the athletic department phones.

There's another situation that you have to be aware of. Think about the telephone technique used in the office that the recruit will be calling. If they call in and the person answering the phone has no idea what's going on, that's working against your recruiting efforts. Recruiting is such a fragile process. Everything has to be perfect, or near perfect. It has to be a 10 on a scale of one to 10. Check out your whole situation. Check your telephone, the person answering the telephone, find out what they say and how upbeat and how professional they sound.

Make sure your confidence level is at the top, too. One of the toughest things is working at your recruiting after you've just lost a game the night before. You've got to keep yourself "up" — moving and motivated — because if you don't walk tall, and do that everyday, then you've got a big-time problem as far as your recruiting is concerned.

Next, identify who you're recruiting against. Try to discover their "Achilles' heel." Then attack, but in a positive manner. You

might be recruiting for a small school. The size of your school might be the one thing that may help you win over a prospect. Consider distance. When you target a prospect, if you can find out information legitimately, do so. Nowadays so much about recruiting is not legitimate. I don't mean it's underhanded; I mean it's not legitimate in regard to the answers that you're going to get when you start asking questions. Particularly at the higher level of recruiting, from the player who's been recruited heavily, you're going to get "standard" answers. You ask, "What are you looking for in a school?" He answers, "I want a great education," or "I want a small school." Then he ends up going to a school with 50,000 students.

Is this honest? No, of course not. But these players sometimes get tired of being asked the same question over and over again. They stop trying to sound original and they just tell you what you want to hear. And who can blame them?

Do Your Homework

I think that you have to really study and study and study. Information gathering is a continuing process, just like recruiting is 12 months out of the year. There's no vacation for your staff because you're continually recruiting. That's going to determine your success.

> **"Create a checklist for phone calls so you make sure you cover all your major points."**

Use your strengths and then continue to sell those. I think your telephone technique and comments with the recruit have to be recorded. You have to have a telephone sheet. Maybe not a script, but perhaps a checklist of the major points you need to cover and your prospect's response. You have to write down what you talked to this person about, what was the point of emphasis and, more importantly, what he told you. Because you're seeking information. Most of the time, you're giving out information. You're talking first and giving out information about your school. You are selling. Change tactics in your follow-up calls. Get that person who's being recruited (or the parents) to talk to give you an idea of what they're looking for.

You have to keep your eyes and ears open and try to get as much information as you can on a prospect, from whomever you can get information from. The next thing is to identify the decision-makers. Is it the mother? You never know who it might be. Whoever it is, you have to help them help the prospect make the final decision and enlist their help in closing the sale.

Who else is looking at your prospect? One of the problems we ran into at Northwestern, and that we ran into at Duke, was the size of the schools recruiting these players. When we identified our competition, it was always UCLA, North Carolina, Notre Dame, the home state school, and Duke. Those were the five that it generally came down to. That's pretty tough competition for men's basketball. That was what we were up against.

We had to keep emphasizing the positive things to our recruits and not say things like, "Duke's too tough for you" or "Northwestern's too tough." We didn't want them to think they had to spend all their time studying, and that they can't work at the game. You also have to find out what your prospect is thinking and saying about you. You can do that but you have to work at it. What are they legitimately criticizing your program for? Find out what the criticism is and who is saying it. It can be the player's classmates or teammates. They may be asking your player, "Why are you going to Duke?" It's 1,000 miles away. They want to know, "Why are you going to this place? Is it because of distance?" Or is it because he is the only one going there from that school.

You have to know what you're up against and how important the person is who is making the statement is to the player. If it's a mom who has the questions, that has more weight than a teammate, although every question gives your prospect a reason to doubt your program and why he or she should choose it.

Don't Guarantee Anything You Can't

> **"Only make promises you can keep."**

I think most private schools are approximately 12% in-state students, 88% out-of-state. I think your recruiting efforts reflect that, and your team reflects that. You have to know what's important to that person and the people surrounding them. What's important? Size of school, distance, or how about playing time? No matter which sport you recruit for, that's becoming increasingly more of a problem. Another problem is the promises other coaches make. I've visited players who say that another coach promised him that he will play 32 minutes a game. My response to that is, "You know what? You'll play 35 minutes a game at our place, if you can guarantee me you're going to get 35 points a game, 20 rebounds and have 10 assists." I make him guarantee me triple doubles, because I can't guarantee playing time anymore than he can guarantee me that he'll have a triple double every game. You sort of make a joke out of it.

A coach can't do that. Throughout my career, I have emphasized to my coaching staff, please don't go out and make rash promises because they're going to come back to haunt us. By the time it comes back to haunt me, the coach who made the promise might be an assistant at another school and I'm the guy who has to coach this kid.

The other point that I make when somebody asks me about playing time is that suppose next year I go around and tell everybody they will play for 35 minutes. Pretty soon, I'm going to run out of players and run out of minutes. It wouldn't be fair to you if I made that promise to you, because everyone else would expect the same thing. I want you playing because you deserve to play, not because I'm keeping track of the minutes I owe you. I also tell them to look very carefully at a program that promises you so many minutes — because that's a promise that's hard to keep. In some cases, for example, if you have a position player who is graduating, you can do everything *except promise him* that he is the candidate for that position — and that may equal significant playing time. If your playing roster is advantageous in your recruiting, show it to the prospect and his parents. It's easier in a sport like basketball because we have 13 players, and I can show a prospect that I have five seniors who will be graduating. If I have two point guards leaving, that leaves me with no point guards. He's a candidate.

Recruiting is getting more complicated. We're fielding questions in basketball that include, "How many shots is he going to get a game?" Isn't that ridiculous? The time has come for changes in recruiting. When you start getting questions like that, it's just unbelievable.

Recruiting is a Science

You better have your on-campus visit down to a science, making sure that it is organized and that your own personnel and your players are involved. Your players are going to sell the program. You have certain players who will do a great job with this responsibility. Other players will do an average job. Who are you going to assign to talk to your best prospects who are coming in? You had better

> **"The better your recruiting *system* is, the more effective you will be in recruiting."**

know, and you had better plan so there are no surprises. The pairings you make should be a science, not a luck-of-the-draw, spur-of-the-moment decision.

Another important part of the campus visit is that you have to allow the parents to know where the prospect is going to be, especially where they are staying. We have a written report we send to the parents which includes who the prospect is going to be talking to. We also try to make sure prospects get a proper balance of being with other players, meeting the people they will be working with, while still working within the rules, because the rules don't allow alumni to be involved on campus anymore. You also want to make sure that you have the proper academic support. You may want to try to take them through what a first year would be like at your particular school. What courses they would take, what the requirements for their degree (if they've chosen one) would be. One of the first things we sometimes do is to go to the guidance office before we go anywhere else.

First things first. In the past we had figured out that of the top 100 men's basketball players in the nation, we could recruit sometimes 18 to 22 of the top 100. We don't want to spend our time recruiting the 75 that can't get in. That's targeting. Don't waste your time on those who can't get in because of academic issues or other constraints. Send them a letter wishing them good luck.

Follow-Up, Follow Through

> **"Even if you don't get the prospect, get his or her feedback so you can improve."**

Constantly work to improve your recruiting system. Do you follow up with the recruits that didn't choose your program to find out why they didn't come to your school? It's something I've never liked to do. I don't like being rejected, and following up with recruits reminds me of that. I did it at Rutgers because the athletic director said I had to. I didn't feel I got fair answers from the players.

Without fair responses, you can't use that information. You need ideas which can really help you in the future. In the past, we've used a written questionnaire. We'd like to have them fill it out and send it back. I think you have to try to find out and hopefully you'll find that you're getting legitimate responses.

Keep learning. I think anytime you see a book out there that can teach you how to work smarter, you should purchase it, because I think that's what recruiting comes down to. I think a lot of people <u>work</u>. I think working <u>smarter</u> is the key. Know what your strengths are, and do more of that. What you don't do well, let someone else do.

One of the hardest things, when you are hired at a new school, is finding out information about that school. My advice is to go right away to the alumni office. Then go to the school's public relations office. Find out who the alumni are, especially the prominent alums. You have to find out from the strengths of the school from every source available. Go to every place that you can think of to find out the strongest selling points. Also, with players you have assisting you with campus visits, I think you periodically have to have seminar sessions with them, so they don't lose sight of what their role is. They are having a certain experience and you want to make sure they know not to tell a prospect things that might be negative, things that a prospect might never even encounter (like certain classes or certain professors). When we study the people that we recruited who came to our school, especially those who were highly recruited, we like to know what areas were really significant in this person's decision. Then we make sure we fix those things that either weren't mentioned or that the player says, "I almost didn't come here because of *x* or *y*."

One other thing is that when you start contacting people at your prospect's school, let them know the positive things that your school has to offer. So much of this contact has to be done by mail. Some of it can be done by telephone and I think that's a very, very important part, if you have the time and personnel. Telephone contacts are harder to make — which makes them more valued than mailers.

Scholarships are another area of concern. You may have one scholarship, but you have five people all vying for it. You have to set a time limit — and tell them, "We have to know in three days." This is what we do in early recruiting, and that's part of our targeting efforts. You've got to work to get your best prospect who is going to choose your school. A lot of that means working smart and trying to get an edge and then having some luck at the end to get that decision to go in your favor.

Pay Attention to the Little Things

There are a lot of little things that you can do, for example, with your letterheads and slogans and sayings. Whatever you do, it should be repeated, repeated, and repeated some more. The use of color and things like that, which can be done legally, whether it be using your school colors, and purple envelopes or whatever. I think it's all important.

> **"Consistency and repetition are both important."**

One area in which I'd stress caution is with phone calls. You have to be very, very sure that when you're making phone contact, it's for a reason. There should be one reason that we can put down on our phone sheets. One piece of paper and one reason for each phone call. In my case, I would go through the listing of previous phone contacts before I'd call someone again. Before I'd schedule a home visit, I would go through that prospect's folder and review all the times we contacted him and why. I'd look at the questionnaire that the player filled out. It's in that folder, too. The questionnaire is important. You've got to get as much information as you can about the player on that questionnaire. Know where the parents went to school and where the high school coach went to school.

Quality is more important than quantity, although in recruiting right now quantity is very important too, particularly in direct mail and getting information out to prospects. You have to continue to study and seek new ideas. I think the saying, "The road to success is always under construction," also applies to recruiting.

Scheduling Your Campus Visit

When you are recruiting against Cadillac programs, and you are fortunate enough to schedule a campus visit, timing can be a big factor. A lot of people wonder if they should be the first visit or the last or somewhere in the middle. We had always tried to be the last campus visit, although it depends on the calendar year, but we tried to fit ourselves in right before the signing period. Although we've tried to be the last one, we've been hurt by that at times. What's happening now is that the better schools are getting commitments by early September, so I've changed my thinking a little bit on that. I'd like to be first now. What's happening is that prospects are visiting the first school and that school is saying, "You're one of our top three choices." If that player has a great visit, he goes home and talks to his parents and is thinking about the next visit. Then, school number one calls and says, "It's getting close. We want you and if you want us, let's make a decision now." That's what's happening. The selling process has been speeded up, and so lately I've been looking more toward being the first or second visit because of what can happen. Particularly if you targeted that player as your best recruit, I'd try to get them in first. Recognize, however, that you can't always be their first or second visit. But it can't hurt to ask. You need to be well organized and you should also be planning ahead because everybody is trying to do that same thing. You're going to have to start planning ahead for your important dates now. You used to be able to do that the last week in August. Forget that. It's too late. Now you are looking at early September visits. I think you have to push the calendar up to July.

All Things Are Not Equal

> **"Accentuate the positives; eliminate the negatives."**

At a small school, you probably don't have a huge team room or an incredible weight room. You may be wondering how your campus visit can even compare with the facilities of larger schools who have the glitz and everything going for them. I think that we're all involved with keeping up with the Joneses — trying to improve our weight room, and all these other areas. I think you have to use size to your advantage. Emphasize that at your school, they're a person, not a number.

Play up what you <u>do</u> have to offer. If your prospect is interested in getting a top-notch education, show them the library. Maybe your library is better. Maybe your weight room is not going to be as good, but you have other things to offer. Somehow you've got to come up with a positive aspect to emphasize. Maybe your weight room isn't as big, but your strength coach is the best in the area. The strength coach works with you one-on-one. That's something we have to offer.

Frame the discussion from a standpoint that the player will receive more personal attention. What's more important? Having a big building that you share with 100 people, or having a personal strength coach who is going to work with you throughout your career. It's not all facilities. For example, at Duke, our crowd capacity was 8,200. Compared to other schools, we're the smallest. Instead of the image that prospects would be playing in huge arenas, we sold the home crowd, the homey experience. We sell the image that you ought to try to play here sometime as an opponent. This is a tough place to play as an opponent, and a tough place to win, because of the students. Even though they're a small crowd, the noise is unbelievable. We sell the noise and the crowd. We sold people there. Prospects can imagine their name reverberating as the crowd chants their name. We didn't sell facility. That's creativity in recruiting.

Are You In The Running?

It can be difficult to know if you're in the running sometimes. I get asked the question, "How do you know if you're in a prospect's top five?" I think the answer to that is to <u>ask</u> <u>them</u>. In your phone calls, you have to ask them, "Are we in your top five?" If you don't want to ask directly, I'd say, "It really sounds like we're one of your top two schools, or your top five schools," and see what they say.

Be sure to write down the answer on your phone sheet as a reminder to you that you've asked the question, and that you've identified what the selection process for that individual is going to come down to. Then you have to try and determine where those people are. Targeting is also a factor here.

As I look back at my career at Northwestern, the highest ranked recruit that we signed, we had identified as the top good man that we felt that we could recruit who would help us. Next, we had to sell him on including us as one of his top choices. We identified him early and we found out what schools he was interested in. We knew that academics really meant something to him and that he loved Chicago. He loved the Cubs and he had an aunt nearby who had also attended Northwestern. They had a great relationship. He knew that he could visit his aunt any weekend or weekday night. It was important to him, and that helped us stay in his top five.

I think that we did a good job recruiting him because we targeted his interests. The fact that we found out that we were one of his top four schools, and then we became one of three. Then we really pushed the Chicago aspect and the fact that his aunt was nearby helped us recruit him. In fact, his aunt made herself and her house available to him when he came.

Keys to Success

The most important keys to success are organization and planning and having a game plan, and then studying your prospect. I can't emphasize this enough. You've got to study and keep yourself alert and keep going because you don't know when you're going to find little bits of information from talking to people that might be a key in signing that recruit.

Start identifying <u>now</u> who your top person is at each position that you can recruit, and get on the phone and try to nail down that campus visit for that first weekend in September. Because if you're not, there are 20 other schools trying to nail down those first couple of weekends.

If you want to be able to compete with the big guns, you need to think small:

- <u>Small victories</u> — being considered as one of your prospect's top five choices.
- <u>Small steps</u>. Gathering information through a series of contacts and recording that information for future use.
- <u>Small advantages</u> — one-on-one coaching and strength training.
- <u>Small classes</u> — If academics are important, emphasize personal attention and small classes.
- <u>Small successes</u> — selecting a campus visit for early September.

Author Profile: Bill Foster

Bill Foster is a 30-year recruiting veteran of Division I and II and is currently a consultant to the commissioner of the Big 12 Conference. A master builder of college teams, Bill is also a member of the Basketball Hall of Fame. Coaching stops included Bloomsburg State, Rutgers University, University of Utah, Duke University, University of South Carolina and Northwestern University. After retiring from coaching, he became athletic director at Northwestern and has also held the position of associate commissioner of the Southwest Conference.

HOW TO RECRUIT THE FRANCHISE PLAYER AT ANY LEVEL

by Billy Hahn

We're always trying to find an edge in recruiting whether we're after the franchise player, or any player really. I just finished my twenty-second year in college coaching. In 22 years of recruiting, no two years have ever been just the same. Ever. It changes every year. It changes because of rules. It changes because of the kind of people you're recruiting. It changes because of the era in which you're recruiting.

I couldn't recruit the same way in the 1990's as I did when I started out in 1975, my first year on the road. I was just a young guy from Morris Harvey College in Charleston, West Virginia. I drove hour after hour after hour in the great State of West Virginia to places I couldn't believe I ended up in. If I recruited the same way today that I recruited then, we wouldn't sign anybody.

The Challenges Facing Recruiters

As an example of the challenges of recruiting in the 1990's with the media and public attention involved, every year the Baltimore Sun writes about our recruiting efforts at the University of Maryland. One of their writers, Mr. Ken Rosenthal, looks at our team and says we had a bad recruiting year. We only signed three guys. None of those players was rated in the top 100 this year. Where's the franchise player in that? This article is about signing franchise players and in our hometown newspaper we get trashed for not signing franchise players.

Our franchise player might be one of the players listed who is not in the top 100. You never know where your franchise player is going to come from. You don't know which one he or she is. Rankings are subjective. Scouting services are guys making money on teenagers. We pay attention to what they say and write because they are self-proclaimed experts in recruiting and evaluating. When they list the top 50 players in the country, we all take notice. But the list is just their opinion. It's not fact. How can you possibly list the top 50 players in the country? It's not possible. Those articles get my attention. I take criticism of our recruiting personally.

Recruiting Becomes a Part of You

You have to take your recruiting personally. You have to wake up every morning with recruiting on your mind. If you don't wake up thinking about recruiting, you're not going to be very good at it. It has to be in your blood. It has to get you excited. You have to stay motivated to recruit. It is a brutal, tough, hard, dirty, and sometimes ugly business. If you think about recruiting any other way, then you need to find something else to do with your life. You have to get up every morning, 365 days a year, and think about what you are going to do to recruit that day. You have to be possessed with it. Of course, that's just my opinion.

I was born and raised on a farm in Indiana. In 1971, I was recruited by one of the best recruiters in America, Lefty Driesell. He came to Mishawaka, Indiana, to recruit this little farm boy who practiced for hours everyday in the barn.

In my house that day were Lefty Driesell, George Raveling and Jim Maloney. They walked in with their coats and ties. I was sitting there with wide eyes as they walked in wearing beautiful tailored suits.

I knew then that if I didn't have a chance to continue to play basketball, that someday I wanted to get into coaching and I wanted to go in and try to recruit. Something about those three gentlemen walking in that house just struck me. If I never had a chance to play again, I wanted to someday coach. And that's what I've done.

I've been very fortunate in this business. I graduated from the University of Maryland and I went to Morris Harvey College in Charleston, West Virginia. What does this have to do with recruiting a franchise player? It gives you my background, how I was born and raised and in the 22 years I've been recruiting, how I had to adjust.

Flexibility and Adaptability Are Keys to Success

> "Each day you are involved in recruiting, you are getting better at what you do."

You have to adjust every year in your recruiting process. You can never stay the same. You are either getting worse or you're getting better. You're not as good today as you were yesterday or tomorrow. Yesterday's gone. Today is today. Tomorrow you don't know what's going to happen, so you better become better today.

And guess what? You're all becoming better today. You've made a commitment. You're trying to get better. That's an important step.

I left the University of Maryland in 1975 and I was recruiting my first year for Morris Harvey College in Charleston, which is now the University of Charleston. We recruited so many franchise players there that they had to change the name of the school from Morris Harvey to the University of Charleston. No, that's not the reason they changed the name of the school.

I can relate to the challenges of recruiting in Division II and Division III schools. I've been there before. Now I'm at a Division I school, in the ACC. I'll tell you what, when you're in Division II, Division III or junior college recruiting, your recruiting efforts are not on the front page of the newspaper like ours are.

I'm fortunate that I've been at a few different kinds of levels. From Morris Harvey I went to the University of Davidson in North Carolina. It's a very similar school to

Princeton. They call it the Ivy League of the South. It's amazing how many schools call themselves "the Ivy League of something." We call the University of Maryland "the Ivy League of Washington, DC."

Developing the Edge in Recruiting

We sell our honors program at the University of Maryland, which is a tremendous program. You better find the edge that your program possesses if you're recruiting that top-notch student-athlete who is also being recruited by Ivy League schools. Our edge is our honors program, which is very, very good.

> "Identify the particular strength of your program."

At Davidson College, which had high academic standards but a low recruiting budget, I drove 98,000 miles recruiting, driving a Ford LTD. I was the third assistant at the program. I'd just gotten married and I was home during the months of December and January just two nights. That was in an era when you could recruit year round.

One time, I drove to Long Island, New York to recruit a kid named Stan Wilcox. Danny Nee had flown in there; he was at Notre Dame at that time. They had a budget. He flew in there, and he had his nice suit on. I had one coat, one tie, and a shirt. I left the next morning, because I had to drive home. Danny was flying back to wherever he was going. It was a quarter to six in the morning and I had to get a jump on things to get out of there on time. I was getting in the car and I put my sneakers on and a sweatsuit. Danny was still sleeping. I tried to sneak out of there in the dark.

When I left the hotel, I left the only pair of street shoes I owned. Later, Danny called me up and said, "Billy, you left your shoes here. Do you want me to send them to you in the mail?"

I said, "Yeah, get them to me as soon as you can Danny, because that's the only pair of shoes that I have."

It was the truth. Danny said, "Billy, do you really want these shoes? The right shoe is disgusting. It has no heel on it, it has no back to it. Are you really going to go recruiting in these shoes?"

I said, "Danny, that's the only pair of shoes I can afford right now. I really need those shoes." He sent me that old beat-up pair of shoes in the mail so I could continue to recruit. Danny and I laugh about that story a lot.

Recruiting has changed a lot since then. From there I went to the University of Rhode Island, and then I joined Ohio University and worked with Danny Nee. I was Danny's assistant for six years. Then I became the head coach at Ohio University. It was my dream. I was pumped up. I was excited. They said at that time I was the third youngest head coach in Division I basketball.

It was the best. My family was proud. But I got so wrapped up in the head coaching spot that I wasn't as good at recruiting as I had been as an assistant.

When you're the head coach, you can't put in the energy and all the time it takes to recruit effectively. ☐I really believe that. So you better have unbelievable people around you if you're the head coach. You better have a staff that wakes up and goes to bed thinking about recruiting.

After three years as the head coach at Ohio University and being a .500 coach, I had a meeting with our athletic director on March 9th. I can remember it like it was yesterday. I walked in his office thinking that he was going to evaluate our season. He sure did. He said, "We're making a change."

He said to me, "You're not going to be here next year." I was in and out of his office in 10 minutes. To this day, I still don't know why he let me go. Believe it or not, all that did was just get me a little bit more excited about being in this business.

Getting Up When You've Been Down

I usually achieved beyond my potential as a player and as a coach. But I've also been knocked flat. I can talk about it now and it's actually good to talk about it because it's made me a better person. I had to start recruiting again, but I had to recruit a different kind of people then. I wasn't recruiting athletes, I was recruiting for a job. Recruiting for the game of life. We all recruit. We recruit everyday.

The good Lord was looking out for me one more time because Gary Williams, now at the University of Maryland, left Ohio State and took the University of Maryland job and where I had played. So I tried to get the assistant coaching job there. He hired me and I've been with him for nine years.

We took a program that was completely down-and-out, on probation, and not on television. We couldn't even play in the ACC tournament.

Now, nine years later, you can't buy a season ticket for University of Maryland basketball. You can't buy a ticket on game day. The games are usually sold out.

We have had four NCAA appearances in a row, and two appearances in the Sweet Sixteen in a row.

Attitude is Everything

You all have your stories, too. You all came from somewhere. Don't ever forget how good you are. Every one of you. You must understand, if you ever think you're not great, then do something to make yourself think you are great.

I can tell you everything about recruiting the franchise player, but none of it matters if you don't have an unbelievable inner feeling about yourself. I'm not talking about being cocky.

Get excited every morning when you wake up. Remember how fortunate you are. I know this may not seem to have anything to do with recruiting the franchise players, but it has a lot to do with it. I have an unbelievable attitude about going out to recruit when I have the opportunity to recruit.

Yeah, it's a tough business. It's hard. But you know what? If you're not excited about it and you don't get excited every morning when you wake up, then you're probably not going to be very good.

You Don't Know What You're Going to Get Until You've Got It

You might think you're recruiting a franchise player and that player might not be worth a darn. You never know what you're going to get in recruiting. You are nuts if you think that. But if you're doing some things ahead of time, ahead of your competition, you have a better chance of finding that franchise player.

> **"Knowing *who* to recruit can be as important as actually recruiting the player."**

A lot of the things I'm talking about, we had done with (former All American) Joe Smith. Joe Smith visited one school. His only visit was the University of Maryland. He was not involved in a "recruiting war." But he ended up being a franchise player.

Somebody always asks me, "Why did you want to get into coaching?" My first year, I was thinking I wanted to get into a coaching job, before I even got to Morris Harvey. I had just graduated from the university in 1975.

Identification is a key factor. So are scouting contacts. Right now everybody's talking about recruiting sophomores and juniors in high school.

Everyday I try to talk to at least one person in my office that can tell me about a sixth, seventh or eighth grade player. You may think I'm nuts, but I'm telling you it works. It's happened over the 22 years of my recruiting.

I've always had a player, wherever I was working, that I was the first one to recruit that person. You can do anything for that kid before he enters the ninth grade, if you know the rules.

Some people say you ought to start recruiting players when they are juniors in high school. They are wrong. You better know who the best players are at the sixth, seventh and eighth grade level. If you have those prospects identified early on, one of them might turn out to be the franchise player.

I want to know how many schools are writing to sixth, seventh and eighth graders. I don't think many are. If a sixth, seventh or eighth grader receives a letter or a note from the University of Maryland, that person is going to remember your institution because that was the first school that contacted them.

You should find an edge. You need to do something different in your recruiting.

Set Yourself Apart from the Crowd

> **"Less recruited prospects will be more receptive to your notes than heavily recruited prospects."**

Don't be a "pack" recruiter, following the lead of the rest of the coaches. In a herd, the whole pack might follow the leader right off a cliff. That's not the way I operate. Every day I could write a particular kid a note. Well, there are a bunch of schools writing to that player everyday. When you get that much mail, that prospect isn't reading every letter. He's throwing it out.

The prospects that read the letters you send them are the ones who aren't being recruited very hard. If yours is the only letter they receive, they are so excited to open that letter up.

I know that is true because when my son was recruited, he wasn't recruited hard at all. He didn't have a single scholarship offer. But I tell you what, when he got a letter from somebody in the mail, it was unbelievable for him because he wasn't receiving many letters. Every letter got his full attention.

I asked some of the players on our team one time what they did with their recruiting letters. They said that they threw them away. They don't even read them.

How to Identify Prospects

Identify early who you're going to recruit. How do you identify those people? First, contact your coaches.

Catholic league coaches might be a possibility. Your contacts – the people that you have out there, are an important source. You should ask them for a favor; ask them to do a little research for you. Let them do some of the legwork for you. Your coaching contacts should include high school coaches, junior high school coaches, Catholic Youth Organization coaches, the Police Athletic League, and AAU coaches are all great potential sources of information.

You'll find that kids at that level, when they're growing up, if they're dominating the other players when they're 10 or 11, not a whole lot will change when they're older.

They will usually continue to dominate as they grow up. Somebody might come along and improve their skills, but you should find out who the players with potential are early.

Another source for identifying prospects is league play. They have basketball leagues everywhere, for all ages. One example is the Police Athletic League, or PAL. You need to find out who the people in charge of the leagues are. Identifying these prospects may only help you recruit one player. But if that one player is a franchise player, it can make all the difference in the world. So you should find out who your key league contacts are and you need to start early.

After You've Identified, Evaluate!

The next step in the recruiting process is evaluation. If you don't have time to go out and see these players when they're young, you need to talk to your contacts and obtain a true evaluation from them. Or have them send you a videotape. You can only be out on the road so many days.

It might be pretty boring to watch a videotape of seventh graders. But you don't have to watch the whole game. You can watch that tape for five minutes and find out who the dominating player is. They stand out in any sport; it doesn't matter.

For example, if you're coaching swimming, it won't take long to figure out who the best swimmer is in seventh grade. He or she is going to win it every time. It's amazing how it works.

If a seventh and eighth grader is struggling in the academic world at seventh and eighth grade, they will continue to struggle in ninth and tenth grade.

When the school finds out a player has a chance to be great, then they'll probably try to give him or her a little bit of extra edge, a little bit more attention. It's amazing how the system works. Those with potential get even more attention, which makes them even better.

Along with athletic ability, you need to find out the academic traits of a prospect. You need to find out what kind of person the kid is. If that prospect is a troublemaker in seventh or eighth grade, then he or she probably will continue to be difficult through high school and college. Creatures of habit are hard to change. It's hard for you to change. It's hard for everyone to change.

That's why the people who become great are the ones who know how to change. You should follow their example. You should change your recruiting techniques. You can't stay the same. You either get worse or you get better. If you are getting worse, then you need to make some changes.

Work Together To Get Better

Share your knowledge, and continue to learn. Who you know can help you improve what you know. Do you ever get together with other coaches at your school and share ideas about recruiting? At the University of Maryland, we don't do that either. I have been trying to get our coaches to get together. You know how many great minds we have? Why can't we find the time to share our techniques and adapt what is most effective? I don't know why, but we haven't been able to.

> **"Don't worry that other coaches are going to 'steal' your best recruiting ideas."**

The University of Maryland's women's lacrosse just won back-to-back national titles. I want to talk to the coach. She won back to back national championships. She might not want to give me her secrets, but I'm going to try to learn from her.

The soccer coach at the University of Maryland turned our soccer program around. He's young and dynamic. I had better go find out how he recruits. I make it a point to talk to people who have been successful. You need to find the edge.

Pick those people's brains. If I think, "I'm the assistant coach at the University of Maryland in the mighty ACC and I know everything," I'm wrong.

You need to find every person you can to give you the edge. That person might be the women's volleyball coach, or the wrestling coach.

Do you know how many great minds are in your athletic department? A lot. Take advantage of what they have learned from trial and error. That will keep you from repeating their mistakes, and you can use what did work to improve your program.

Use "Perimeter People" To Your Advantage

Once you identify those players, you need to find what I call "the perimeter people." How can you identify them? Coaches might know or you might find out from that recruit who the perimeter people are. You're allowed one phone call per week. You're not going to be able to accomplish much of anything with one phone call. So you have to be a great recruiter and use the perimeter people to your advantage.

What are perimeter people? They are all of the people around your prospect. When I walk into a high school to recruit, the first thing that I do is find out who they are. Obviously the coach is key, but the assistant coach is even more important, because they are usually the buffer between the head coach and the players. The assistant coach usually has a better relationship with the players. So immediately find out who the assistant coach is.

A team manager is also a good perimeter person. They tell you everything you need to know about that prospect.

Information Is Your Best Ally

> "The more you know about the prospect, the better you will be able to recruit him or her."

You have to compile information on the player you're recruiting. Find out who his best friend is. What he likes. What are his hobbies. What's his favorite rock group, or rap group? Who is his girlfriend? Who does he hang out with? Who does he go to the mall with? You have to find out who the key people are around him. You need to recruit those people, too. If you know all those people that your prospect talks to on a regular basis, they will hopefully mention your school often and ingrain it into their mind. They can end up selling the university and your program for you. I haven't even discussed the impact that the prospect's mother and father have yet.

Whoever is out there speaking on your behalf, whether it's a coach, a friend, a teacher, or a parent, you're getting a competitive advantage.

If that prospect constantly hears about your school, you have a great chance of signing that player down the road. That is, if you've identified them early enough in the process. Don't forget, our great player Joe Smith only visited one school. He already knew the University of Maryland was where he wanted to go to school. You can get that kind of commitment long before the letter of intent signing date. He made the commitment in his mind before he made the commitment on paper.

Using the Teacher in the Recruiting Process

You should ask every prospect you recruit who his or her favorite teacher is. Then you have to recruit that teacher. You should be sending notes to teachers as well as coaches.

Recruiting is hard. If you're not willing to put in the time, then you might as well forget it. You should get out of bed and think every morning how to get the edge. If I'm sending a note to the teacher, that might be my edge. I don't think very many recruiters are doing that.

"The Here and the Now" is More Important Than History

Last year the media might have trashed our recruiting class. But two years ago, our recruiting class might have been ranked twelfth in the nation by these so-called experts. The year before our recruiting class was eighth in the nation. Our recruiting classes are typically nationally ranked. Now last year, they're trashing us.

> **"You can only get better at what you do, so try to improve for the future."**

Let this be a lesson to you. No one cares what you've done in the past. They want to know, "What have you done for me lately?" I take this criticism very personally. I examine what I am doing differently today than what I did when we were ranked. Maybe I didn't start early enough on this year's recruiting class. Maybe we got a little complacent when we had our nationally ranked classes.

Criticism serves as a wake-up call for me. I use it to improve myself and to improve our program. I re-examine everything. We might let some assistant coaches go. Getting fired is the wake up call of life. Don't get in a comfort zone. How do you know you will have a job tomorrow? You better make sure you have one by doing everything you can to be the best you can be today.

In the recruiting process, identifying the champion is easy after you've done all the labor, work and cultivation. Recruiting is almost like planting. You plant the seed early. You watch the seed grow. The seventh grader is the seed. You're going to eventually harvest the crop but it takes a long time and you have to cultivate it. You need to weed out things.

Identify the Player's "Champion"

> "The 'champion' helps the player make his or her decision."

Eventually you're going to find out who the champion is in the recruiting process. The champion is not the player. The champion is the one person besides the recruit, who is eventually going to help that young man or young woman make their decision. Believe me, every player has a champion. A lot of times the champion works without the young man or young lady even knowing that they are making the decision for them. The player does not always make his own decision. The mom, dad, or coach may say that it's the player's decision, but it's not. So find the champion.

There's one for every player – maybe it's the teacher, the janitor, the uncle, the grandma, the girlfriend, the coach, the mother, or the father. There are a lot of people who can give you clues as to who the champion is, but it is essential to find the champion in the recruiting process.

Once you identify the champion you are going to sign the franchise player. When it gets down to the player's decision, you have to be different. Keep in mind the ways you can be different. Writing that teacher a note is being different.

Use What You Know

Use what you know about the player to your advantage. This goes back to the information you have gathered about him or her.

Talking to a player about a song or if he or she likes a certain musical group is always a nice touch. The player might ask you "How did you know I like that rap group?" You knew because you did your homework with the perimeter people.

I can't emphasize enough how important it is to be different. Have you thought about getting a rubber stamp that says "Important" in big red letters so when you write a note to the prospect you can stamp that on the outside of the envelopes that you send them? How about a stamp that says "You're number one" on the outside of the envelope?

Your prospect is getting mail from all different places. Something has to make yours stand out. How about using a colored envelope instead of a white envelope?

If a player receives 20 letters and there are 19 white ones in there and one red envelope, which one do you think stands out in the crowd?

Now What?

You found the champion. You've done all this work as the recruiter. You've done everything with him. You've cultivated that plant. So much so that it's now time to harvest. If you've done your job properly, you have now become that young lady or that young man's best friend.

> **"Make it hard for a prospect *not* to choose you."**

My goal in recruiting prospects is to make them the most miserable person in the world the day they try to tell me no. A player might still tell you no, even after all that you've been through. They're going to tell you "no" more than they will tell you "yes." You're not going to get them all.

But I'll tell you what, there's nothing better than to see a prospect squirming and being nervous. You can feel it in the voice. That might make it harder for them not to choose your program than one who has done everything right, but isn't as close as you are.

Rely on Facts, Not Intuition

If you're not good on the phone, you better be able to tell what a prospect is thinking. I can almost see through my phone when I talk to a prospect. I know if we're out of the picture just by the tone of voice. You better know their voice.

You've got to make it so you become a friend of the player and a friend of the perimeter people, so that when it's decision-making time, it will be murder for that coach or that kid or that family member to say "no" to you.

That's how you close the deal. You've got to make them suffer. I'm sorry if that sounds rude or mean or malicious. But think about all of the hours, the time, and all of the effort you put into it. If the prospect says "no," then I suffered a lot, too. So get them to the point where they're such a good friend of yours that they can't tell you "no."

The keys to recruiting the franchise player are simple:
- Set yourself apart from the crowd.
- Identify prospects early on in their development – they're never too young for you to look at them.
- Enlist other people to help you recruit – coaches, teachers, parents, friends.
- Find the person or people who will help the player make his or her decision.
- Make it hard for that prospect to tell you no.
- On a personal level, never stop learning.
- When you stop being excited about the recruiting process, it's time to get out.
- Learn from the mistakes of others.
- Make mistakes, but don't make them more than once.
- Let criticism motivate you to do better, not to become bitter.

Just remember, you all have to have an edge today. Recruiting the franchise player is no easy task. You're trying to get ahead of somebody. Don't ever stay the same. Be creative. Let your mind flow. Think. Brainstorm. Be different. You can't stay the same or you'll be out of the game.

Everyone has the same rules. You all get the same one phone call per week. Dare to be different. Think of something – within the boundaries of NCAA rules – that you can do to set yourself apart. That's what will help you recruit your franchise player.

Author Profile: Billy Hahn

Billy Hahn is assistant men's basketball coach at the University of Maryland. Tabbed by many national publications as one of the top recruiters in the country, he has been instrumental in the rise of Maryland basketball to national prominence. Other coaching stops include Morris Harvey College, Davidson College and the University of Rhode Island. He has also held both assistant and head coaching positions at Ohio University.

EFFECTIVE PHONE RECRUITING TECHNIQUES

by Sheilah Lingenfelter

Whether you've been recruiting by phone for 10 days or 10 years, most coaches would say that they don't enjoy this particular part of the recruiting process. Phone calls are the tough part about recruiting. In this article, I'm going to present some ideas to help make phone recruiting a little bit easier for you, or at least maybe make it less frustrating for you.

What is so important about phone calls is that everyone's doing it these days. And if you're not doing it — if your program's not doing it — then you get asked the question by prospects, "Why didn't you call me?" Peer pressure is the key here. If you are a prospect, and one school is calling you once a week and other schools are calling you every other week, and there's another school that's not calling you at all, that last school probably won't sign you unless you've already got a tie to the school, or you like the school's name or the program. Even if you don't like phone recruiting, there are a lot of things that you can do to help yourself and make the process less frustrating.

Know the Rules

The first place you have to start is learning the recruiting rules for your division, your conference, and your sport. Ignorance is not a defense. You can get in big trouble with what you're doing or what you're trying to do, even if you didn't know it was wrong.

I like the phrase, "The art of conversation." I think that is exactly the way to describe an interpersonal, verbal interaction. It truly is an art, not a science. Many times, you're having a forced conversation with a total stranger — trying to grab their attention right from the start and keep it all the way through. You're trying to keep their interest. You're trying to get them to want to learn more and know more about your program. The other thing that makes these conversations tough is that you're probably talking to an adult and a teenager at the same time.

Unfortunately, many of us haven't been in a teenager's shoes for quite some time and sometimes we don't know what they're going through. We don't understand what it is like to be besieged by information and by people who call and want to be their best buddy. Unfortunately, sometimes the things that they're going through nowadays are things that we didn't have to go through when we were growing up. There are a lot of factors that this teenager may be considering that you don't even know about. It might be a good idea to try to find these things out while you're having a conversation with him or her.

A five-minute conversation can seem like an eternity when you're talking with someone who is making it tough. What I mean by that is the five-minute conversation that seems like it's taking about an hour, because you're asking questions and talking and the only response you're getting is, "Uh-huh, uh-huh."

Sometimes that's because the prospects are overwhelmed by the whole situation. Sometimes it's just that they are shy and not used to talking about themselves and verbalizing their goals and their dreams. They might be a little bit withdrawn naturally.

Maybe it's that they are not used to having people calling them up.

On the other hand, you might get prospects who think that everyone in the world should be calling them and if you're not spending the time with them that they think they deserve, then they say, "See ya later." These tend to be "me-oriented" conversations. It's not "What you can add to our program," but "What's in it for me." So you really have to know the type of person that you're dealing with before you call. That way you can be prepared, not only for the length of the call that you expect, but how much of the talking you'll have to do.

Plan Ahead and Be Organized

There are some organizational things that will help you, especially on that first call. First, it is important to jot some things down as you talk to the prospect. Second, you should have some type of a rough script that you're going to use. When I'm talking about rough script, I'm talking about a written outline that you can be spontaneous with.

You know what it's like when you get a perfectly scripted phone call that's completely impersonal. I can usually tell if they mispronounce my name. For example, they call and say, "I'd like to speak with S. A. Ling Lingen...felter, please." What do you immediately do? Hang up. See ya later. You tune them out right from the start.

Get the little things right. Know the prospect's name; know how to pronounce it (correctly!), and know what they'd like to be called, whether it's a nickname or a given name. If there's somebody who has an extremely difficult name and you do not know how to pronounce it, call their coach first. Call their guidance counselor first. Call somebody. Don't wing it on the first call. Because if you dial the phone and you say, "I'd like to speak with um," that's a bad first impression. And you know, you never get a second chance to make the right first impression. Don't take chances — do your homework. Who knows all the weird names that kids go by now. It might be as simple a name as Suzanne and she goes by Susie.

The other thing you can do to avoid name trouble is to add a line to the questionnaires that you send out, asking for "preferred name." Then use that name when you're calling.

If you don't know the pronunciation of that kid's name, then go to another source. It will only take you one minute to find out from another source what your prospect likes to be called and how his or her name needs to be pronounced.

Make Sure You Cover the Key Topics

Another key point is that you should divide your phone strategy into key topics. These are the main things you'll be talking about when you are on the phone with a prospect. Key topics fall into three general categories.

> **"Know what information you want to get from the prospect in the phone call."**

One category includes all the school information you need to exchange, such as the location of the school (yours and his or hers) and where the prospect is located geographically in relation to where you are geographically. Many times, when you are calling a prospect for the first time, they have no clue if you're in the state or if you're out of state. Sometimes, unfortunately, they have no idea where your state is located.

The second category is presenting the level of play. That is, what division you are. You may want to present all the advantages that your institution has over other schools. Also, find out if they are playing other sports at the current time. Maybe they're not interested in playing basketball at your school, but maybe they're in the middle of their basketball season, so you can find out how that's going. If you really want to make a difference – and this has more to do with in-person recruiting than phone recruiting – there's nothing that's more impressive sometimes than to show up at one of the games, even if it's not something that you coach.

Finally, the third category is all of your team things. You could talk for hours about how wonderful your team is, about the great support personnel that you have and your excellent facilities.

It's funny that while you can talk for hours on what you *do* have that the other schools *don't*, you always tend to leave out the things that you *don't* have that you know they *do* have down the street. That's okay. Showcase your strengths. There's no use pointing out your weaknesses. A prospect who does his or her homework will know those weak points anyway.

Show Me The Money

The other thing prospects are interested in is the bottom line. Be prepared to talk money. They want to know what you can offer financially – that is, scholarships – right away. If you can't give them that information right away, at least give them a general overview or tell them where they can go to find out that information.

I know initial phone contacts aren't usually when you immediately start talking scholarship information, but at least you can let them know the tuition and fee costs of your institution and what resources are available for them and what the general financial picture is for your school, whether you are Division I, Division II, NAIA or Division III.

You are their expert. You are their resource. You have to know the Division rules and procedures from A to Z. You *cannot* lead these families astray, even though a lot of the financial information will remain open-ended and unanswered until later in the recruiting process.

There is really one other major thing that we need to do more as coaches. Even when we have a script, when we've written out all the information that we want to present, we've got to listen more. As a coach, sometimes we have all this information to share and we just want to present, present and present, and we don't find out anything about the prospect. We spend maybe 10 or 15 minutes talking with a prospect.

What percentage of that 10 minutes are you talking and what percentage are you listening? We have two ears and one mouth. Use that proportion as your guide. Spend twice as much time listening as you do talking. For a 10-minute conversation, that means 6-7 minutes listening and only 3-4 minutes talking.

Sometimes we cram a bunch of information down a prospect's throat for half an hour and then just end the conversation. We waste the opportunity to try to find out more about the prospect – their dreams, their goals, their roots, their background, and their interests. With every single phone call, you should be finding out something about the prospect you're talking to. When you hang up the phone, you should write down on your call log what you talked about, what you learned, and what you need to follow up on. You need to have accurate records of your phone calls.

> **"Rule #1 is know who you are talking to. Don't confuse one player with another."**

The worst thing you can do is call somebody, find out something and then think to yourself, "That's pretty significant; I'll remember that." And then you say to the wrong kid, "Well, how was the play that you were in this past week?" The confused prospect replies, "I wasn't in a play." The prospect is thinking, "Does this coach even remember who I am?" You're thinking, "Shoot, I blew that one." Write down what you learn during those phone calls. Then you can refer back to it — correctly — in your next conversation with the prospect. Ask, "How did the play go? Or, "How did that English paper end up that you were working on the last time I talked to you?" *That's* showing interest. And yes, it's written down there right in front of you, but it's showing that you care. They don't have to know you wrote it down. For all they care, you could have the memory of the Elephant Man.

With a lot of these kids, maybe you do show or have the potential to show that you care about the player as a person. In fact, you may show that you care more than anyone about what they're dealing with day to day, right now in the home that they're living in, or in the school that they're going to or in the programs that they're playing for.

I know that sounds pretty extreme but some of these players out there are in pretty bad situations. Some of them out there are looking for a chance to get out, to start new, to start fresh and to have somebody care about them. Whether you want that kid in your program is up to you. But that's something that we need to be aware of as coaches.

Remember – Players Are Also People

It's so easy sometimes to get caught up in a player as an athlete that we lose sight of them as a person. So what we are doing, is compounding that problem. If you only talk to that player about, "How many points did you score last night?" Well, when's your next game?" and then you say, "Well, I have to go." That's losing sight of them as a person. If you say, "Hey, the last time we talked, you had just scored 25 points. How many did you score this time?" and "What's your record now?" and "When's your next game?" and then you hang up. The player is going to get the idea that all you care about is the sport and the athlete and not the person.

> **"Find out about your prospects both as a *player* and as a *person*."**

Find out more about your player than just about the game. There's more to their lives than that. And there's a lot more in the future of their lives than that.

Prospects Are Judging You, Too

When you are on the phone with someone, if they're interested in your program, they are taking mental notes of what you're like, too. They're figuring out in their mind, "What's this coach like? Are they open? Do they seem open? Do they seem honest? Are they evasive? Are they good about answering all of my questions? Do they really seem interested, or are they only looking for one thing?" After all, you're making the same judgments about that person on the other end of the line.

I know there's times when I should not be calling prospects, even if it was on my "to do" list for the day. If I had an absolutely miserable day and the thought of being in that office for two hours or three hours more, making calls is the last thing I want to be doing. If you feel like that, well, don't do it that day.

If you're just rushing through your calls just to try to get through them, put it off and do it another day. Or get someone else in your program to do it. Or suck it up for the two hours like we sometimes make our athletes do. We say, "Hey, I know you failed those tests. I know you've had a bad day, but this is practice. Get out there and give it your all."

Maybe that's what we need to do when we don't feel like making the calls. We've got to get enthusiastic and we've got to try to sell it. That's the only way that we're going to continue to attract good students and get those blue chippers that we all need in our program, because we're all fighting for them. After all, we're usually fighting for the same players.

Be "The Man With the Plan"

> "Be prepared to just leave a message."

As you make your calls, have a Plan A and a Plan B. Plan A is what are you going to do or what you are going to say if the athlete is home. Plan B is what you are going to do if that athlete is not home, which tends to be the case more often than Plan A these days. You need to decide ahead of time what you are going to do. What will you do on the first call if no one is there? Leave a message? Hang up and try again? Do you talk to the parents? Decide before you dial.

Do you want the first contact that you have with the student-athlete to be a message left on an answering machine, saying "Call me back?" Probably not, because what's going to happen? A little brother or a little sister gets home first, plays the messages, and then erases the messages and it's long gone.

It isn't until two weeks later when you think to yourself, "This person never got back to me; why not?" Even parents are in such a hurry that sometimes even a parent may forget. That's especially true if two or three coaches are all calling around the same time.

So have a plan for what you're going to do. There's nothing wrong with talking to parents. There's nothing wrong talking with other people in the family. Sometimes that's the only way that you can set up appointments for the next time that you're going to try to get that person. And that's when you know that it's okay to call them after 11:30 at night because that's usually what time they're finally home.

The First Impression

That first call is very important. The reason that it's important is that it is the thing that's starting to open the door. You're getting your foot in the door of that home to reach that student-athlete. On your call sheet, make sure that you leave space for questions. I know a lot of times on first calls, the prospect won't be asking questions. They might have one or two. If the student is prepared, they'll have some. If they have not given it any thought, when you ask, "Do you have any questions?" and they say, "No," that might tell you that maybe this person is not interested in your school, and rather than being impolite, they are just acting disinterested.

So a way to get around the "Do you have any questions," question is ask *them* questions. For example, "What are you looking for in a school? What area would you like to go to? What size school are you looking for? What division is important to you? Would you like to play more than one sport in college?"

There are so many questions and maybe some of them have just a yes or no answer, but at least it helps pull them into the conversation. Sometimes that might loosen them up so that they might begin to ask other questions.

Another objective you try to achieve with a phone contact is not only trying to get them interested in your school, but to get them physically on your campus. Sometimes that takes many phone calls. Other times, it may just take a couple. But the main objective is to physically get that person to your campus. Whether it's a paid visit, official visit, unofficial visit, unpaid visit, or whatever, just get them there. Even if it's just a matter of having them come to one of your games and then meeting them before or after it, that's getting them physically on the campus.

Tracking Down Student Applications

After you get them on campus, the next objective is to get their application. Try to talk them into getting those applications in as soon as possible. Then, when they get it in, follow up. It's essential to follow up with the player at this point. Don't just say to yourself, "Hallelujah, the application is here; now we're off and running."

> **"Know where your prospect is in the admissions process at your school."**

You have got to follow up. You've got to be excited about the fact that your prospect has taken that time to fill out the application and send it in. It's especially important if your school has a lengthy or complicated application. A completed application in that case indicates serious interest on your prospect's part.

The major problem in tracking applications is that they aren't sent directly to you. If the prospect is sending the application to the admissions office, you need to know how current your admissions office is in updating their records. This is a problem on some campuses. If you call the player and he or she says, "I sent it in a couple of weeks ago," you look dumb because the admissions department didn't tell you that they had received the application.

To keep from sounding like a fool, try to establish better communication with the admissions department, whether that's just keeping up to date with them through personal contacts about your prospects or logging into their computer.

The next step is the acceptance. It's probably the most vital part of the admissions process. It's that important. Some admissions offices will tell you to make sure your prospect has received the acceptance letter before *you* say anything to them about their acceptance. Some admissions offices tell you that it is all right to call up your prospect and tell him or her that they're accepted, even to call them up and congratulate them on their acceptance. If you do that, you need to also be prepared to discuss the financial aid package. At that point, it's getting down to the wire and they're ready to go, and hopefully, they are ready to start making some decisions.

Sign on the Dotted Line

> "The ultimate point of recruiting is to sign the prospect. Focus on that event."

The other thing that is frustrating about phone calling is trying to get a final commitment from your prospect. Sometimes these students will just string you out while they are waiting for someone better to call. It happens to everyone. Some players will wait and wait and wait for that premier program to call them.

Players and their families do not seem to understand that if you haven't heard from the premier program, then there's no point in running to your mailbox everyday.

The other thing that is so misleading to prospects is that if they get a letter from a premier program, they think that means they're a top recruit for that program. They make that assumption just because they received a form letter sent to them at the beginning of the school year. They haven't heard from the coach. They haven't heard from the assistant coach. And they haven't heard from a player yet. But they are waiting and they're hoping and they know that somehow, that program is going to come through for them.

To try and get the final commitment, I try to make them feel as comfortable as they can talking to me. I will often ask players what their interests are. I will try to get to know them as a person so that I will instill in them the fact that I care what their decision is – even if it's not our program. I will let them know that if they decide to attend another school – if he or she is no longer interested, I'd like to know. I let them know that they can send me a note or they can have a parent call me or they can have someone else call. I care about you. But if you decide to go somewhere else, I just want to know.

I try to communicate, as best as I can, that I won't be mad if they choose to go somewhere else. I will be disappointed, of course, especially if we really made a connection, but they've got to understand that you're going to continue to recruit them and contact them and if they don't want you to keep bugging them, then they need to tell you that they've made another decision.

Players stringing recruiters along is getting to be a major problem in recruiting right now. I don't have any clear-cut ideas on how to minimize it from happening.

Sometimes the worst people to deal with are parents. They're sometimes the ones who are behind the player stringing out a coach. I don't know why – maybe they are doing it because of their ego. They like the fact that their son or daughter is being courted by six or seven schools. Or maybe they are holding out for something better. Maybe the parent was once a player, and they didn't get the Division I scholarship so, "By god, my son or my daughter is going to get it if it's the last thing I do!" My son or daughter is going to get that because I was not good enough to get it. That's a parent trying to live vicariously through a student-athlete. It's something to keep an eye out for.

Using Intermediaries

There are people who can help you who deal directly with our recruit. The first group of intermediaries who can help you make contact is the family and guardians. Unfortunately these days, you don't know who your prospect is living with. Are they living with their two original, intact parents? Are they living with a stepmother? A stepfather? Grandparents? There's so many things that these students are dealing with outside of sports and school – and family situation is a big issue. If you know that, and you understand that, it might help you deal with the family or the student. A family member can be an important ally in making a connection with a prospect. Try to have a good relationship with whomever in the family seems to be the "head of the family" or the decision-maker. Most families have one member who seems to take charge. I'm sure through the recruiting process you're going to end up talking to these people quite a few times. You should treat that person with the same respect you give to the student, because their influence may turn out to be key to your signing that prospect.

The other person that you need to talk to if you're interested in signing a player is the coach. When you're talking about "coach," it's not usually just one person – there are so many coaches now. They have the regular coach of their high school team. They have a summer coach. They have a club coach. They have a specific coach, such as a speed training coach. They may have specific coaches who focus on developing certain skills. A weight training coach.

> **"The involvement of a prospect's coach can be critical in signing that player."**

Be aware of the number of coaches involved. Find out which ones are particularly close to your prospect. If you know a coach is involved, sometimes you are able to pinpoint the coach who has the most influence. See if you can determine that in your phone conversations. Find out who you might want to spend a little bit more time with because that coach might have more of an influence on your student-athlete than his or her parent.

Alumni Are Key Intermediaries

Another group that you need to be aware of are alumni. Know your alumni background. Try to identify people who have played in your program who also went to your prospect's school, or who also played on that club team, or who also worked with that player's specialized coach.

> **"Use your alumni wisely in the recruiting process."**

Alumni present a super way to try to get the attention of a prospect. You can bring your alumni in to give you some insight. Use the alumni as a reference (with the alum's permission, of course). Tell the player and the family, "'So and so' came here and if you have any questions about the program, call them." Many times, especially in small communities, the prospect will know your alumni contact. It can mean a lot to the prospect to have reassurance from someone they know.

The best alumni, of course, are relatives of the student. A parent or sibling can be a great asset in recruiting, but it can also be a big drawback if the student-athlete doesn't want to fill someone else's shoes. So go ahead and use alumni wisely if you know they had a positive experience and that the prospect will react positively to the alumni contact.

The other person you need to consider and to get involved is the prospect's guidance counselor, especially considering some of the statistics available now. That guidance counselor is the person who is making sure that applications are being completed and mailed. Sometimes things will sit on their desk for a couple of weeks because they're trying to handle a lot of things at once. Maybe just one call can help. Introduce yourself and ask (if it's not too much trouble) that when your prospect's application crosses their desk, you'd appreciate their assistance in processing it. Tell him or her, "I just talked to the coach on this one," and you'll often get the counselor's reply of, "I'll get this one right out." Get any help you can get with the application.

The next thing, and I really don't think we use this enough, is our own university support staff. Have assistant coaches call. One article I read said the first couple of calls should be made by the head coach, and the third call should be made by the assistant coach, promoting the head coach a little bit. That's a great idea and if you use a system like that, it can work extremely well.

Consider Using Your Athletes in Phone Recruiting

The last group you can use to help with phone recruiting are the student-athletes. It's especially effective if you've got an athlete from the prospect's geographical area. The thing that you need to be real careful with though is try not to have athletes from the same position that they're going to be playing calling your prospects. You don't want to say, "Well, we really need to get this pitcher," so you have your current pitcher call. It can cause a lot of hurt feelings because now your pitcher thinks they might be sitting on the bench. So you might want to have a catcher call your prospect, or someone else.

Choose someone who can really answer the prospect's questions. It's unbelievable what students will ask other students. Sometimes they won't ask *you* a darn thing. You might then have a student call and then the student will say, "Well, we talked for half an hour. They had a lot of questions." Your prospect may be afraid of an authority figure. But they'll ask another student anything. "What's it like on the weekends? Do people join sororities and fraternities?" They'll ask all kinds of stuff.

You need to be careful if you get into the habit of having students as your only callers. I know there are some programs where students do all the calling. The danger is that the students are the only one that the prospect is ever talking to.

The other danger is that you don't want your students to be so overwhelmed by the whole process that they are feeling like you feel on some days. "Uh, you mean we have to call recruits again today?" You know they are not going to be selling the program. They've already sucked it up for practice, so to have them suck it up for another couple of hours on the phone, might be asking too much. So be careful of using students as your only telephone recruiters.

Work With Your University Departments To Recruit A Prospect

Some other resources who can provide you with some additional assistance are admissions and your financial aid department. You need to be very careful working with these two departments and you need to know what your admissions office is doing. Are they calling your prospects? I know at our university, our admissions office personnel spend a lot of time on the phone. There are sometimes when I might call a prospect and they may have just spoken with someone from our admissions office that day.

> **"Parents want to know how you will prepare their child academically for the future."**

Admissions are getting pretty competitive, and the admissions office will often make contacts of their own to try and recruit individuals to attend the school.

However, if your admissions office is not following through, then you might have to be doing more of the follow-up yourself. But you need to talk to your admissions office and determine how they operate and what their plan is for your contacting recruits.

You also need to find out what mailings are being sent from the university to the student. A good way to follow-up with prospects is if you know that a mailing is going out on a certain date, you can call your prospect a couple days after that and say, "We sent out a mailing and an institutional financial aid form. Did you get it?" Then tell your prospect it is very important to return that form in order to process the financial aid. If you know when mailings are going to be sent, it can improve your phone conversations. It's a matter of timing.

I also don't think we use our own faculty members enough. It's not enough to get faculty members to come to the games. You can enlist the faculty's support by identifying the best candidates to target. Ask the players on your team, 'Who is the best person in the psychology department? Who is the best person in the education department?"

Then you can get that person on your side so that if you get a blue chip player who is interested in that major, you don't have a problem calling the person at your institution and saying, "Hey, we have a great kid here. They have some questions about your area. Could you just call and talk to them for about five minutes? If your faculty will help you out with answering a prospect's questions, it will make an impression on that recruit. You should try to take advantage of all the resources available in the institution.

Sometimes we see ourselves as an island. It's your job to sign that recruit. The bottom line is, when it comes down to signing them or not signing them, a lot of times it comes down to how the prospect feels about the head coach.

On the other hand, there's a lot of other people whose knowledge or resources you can use to take some of the burden off of your head.

Style and Substance

> "Your personal style is perceived to be the school's style, so make sure the two match up."

Your personal style is the biggest key to predicting success in phone recruiting. That's especially true if you're spending more time on the phone and you still haven't been able to get the student to your campus yet.

I think it is really important to keep within your style. If you are a person who is interested in other people, if you tend to be a talker, if you enjoy talking to people, then have that be your style.

If you're a businesslike person who just sticks to the point, then that should be your style. Within your style, you need to be aware of certain things. You can be successful with any style you use. It's what you do with that style and where you take it that are important.

Even when you're on the phone, your prospect can tell if you're being phony. If you ask, "What other colleges are you looking at?" Or, "How is your job going?" Or "How's your mother doing?" and then you only give him or her 30 seconds to answer, because now you're on to the next thing, the prospect is going to know that you're working from a script and you're just trying to get through it.

If you're thinking, "I have 10 more people to call," you're not going to be focusing on this one individual You may not be telling them that, but as you're talking, it's going to come across in your style.

Whatever style you use, make sure that it's sincere and not phony or forced.

The other style that you can have is the "Just the facts, ma'am" approach. You spell it all out. This is what the program is like. This is what the school is like. This is what our students are like. Of course, you're going to expound on all those things. But you live by the facts. This is what it is and this is what it's like and we want you here.

Don't Get Caught Up in the Fantasy

Then there's the fantasy style. People who use this style always have some interesting story. They always really pump up their program, sometimes even more than what it really is.

I think we all use a little of the fantasy style every now and then. Sometimes it's good to do a little bit of both, especially as you progress through the recruiting process. But with the fantasy style, make sure that you're consistent with what you're doing.

You don't want to pump up your program so much that when the person comes to your campus they ask you, "Well, where's this?" and "Didn't you say you had this?" and "I thought you said you had that?"

They'll catch you right away, especially if you think, "Well, I really want this person to consider us as one of their top picks and I don't know if they'll ever come and visit, so I'm going to really inflate the stories because I know they have so many people calling them that they'll forget what I told them." If you want to take that chance, you could get into some trouble with that.

The other coaching style is high pressure. With a high pressure style, the first thing out of the coach's mouth, after they ask the prospect's name and after they identify themselves, is "Have you made a decision yet? Are you coming?" The prospect replies, "Well, no, I still haven't made a decision."

I actually overheard a conversation that went something like that and I couldn't

believe it. The coach and the prospect went through that exchange and then the coach said, "Okay, I'll give you a call next week to see if you've made your decision by then. You know I really want you in our program, but I'm not going to waste your time telling you a lot of things. I've talked to you a lot and you know we want you and I'll call you next week." Click.

Ethics and Negative Recruiting

Finally, I think another issue in phone recruiting now is there is a major problem with ethics. A lot of things can happen on the phone, and this is where it gets started. As coaches, we have to realize that it's easy to slip into negative recruiting, which is really a roundabout way of criticizing another program.

It's unintentional. You don't really mean to do it, or you may mean to do it, but what you think you're doing is positively promoting your program by putting another program down. For example, you might say, "Well, our weather here is awesome. It's sunny all the time. I know a lot of the other schools you're looking at may not be able to play as much because of their weather or they might be playing all their games with sweatshirts on." Or you might say about the other program, "Well, such and such school, they haven't won the conference in five years and we've been conference champions for the last five years." Meanwhile you're not telling them that this other team was second place in the conference for those five years. What you're doing is that you're putting someone else's program down, even if it's in a roundabout way.

> "Negative recruiting is often due to a lack of confidence."

I wish parents and students would realize that when a coach is engaging in negative recruiting on the phone, they don't have confidence in their own program. They don't feel that you can make an educated decision yourself, that you can look at their program objectively, and make decisions based on facts. As a coach, why do I need to belittle this other program? Why can't I just say we were conference champions the past five years? Why do I have to put another program down to make my program look better? This is an area that has been getting a lot of attention recently, and rightfully so. Don't be negative. Hopefully, in the future, we'll see negative recruiting backfiring on the person or program using that technique.

Negative Recruiting and Libel

The second area for ethical concern is making statements that could be potentially grounds for a lawsuit. Libelous statements are when we put down the coaches or the coaching staff, maybe by putting down their personal reputations. Or their religious preferences. Or their win/loss record. Or their coaching ability.

How can you recognize a potentially libelous statement? Statements such as "You know, that program hasn't won a conference in five years" or "That coach has been there for five years and they've never been to the NCAA tournament." Those might not be libelous. But why do we need to say that? Why do we need to talk about players on other teams? Don't say, "You don't want to go there, they smoke all the time." If that's really the case, let the prospect go on a campus visit to that university. They will see it for themselves. Let the prospect do his or her homework on the school they choose. If they care enough about choosing the right program, they will do the research on the coach's win/loss record themselves.

Train Your Student-Athletes to Avoid Negative Statements

Be careful about the things that you tell student-athletes. If you cannot sell your own program without putting someone else down, you should not be doing it. If you cannot sell it, then you have got to educate your staff to do it for you. If you've got players calling, you don't want your players saying, "Oh, man, we kicked their butts! They're terrible!" You've got to educate your entire program with this. Don't just assume that people will know not to engage in negative recruiting.

> "Your staff will follow your example, so make sure you don't set a bad example."

Our student-athletes can be as guilty as anybody to talk about another team, another program, or another coach. But you need to be careful when you have them call. You want them representing your institution and your program. Make sure that they have the philosophy that you want them to have. Give them some ground rules for what you want them to cover.

With as competitive as the recruiting is getting these days, the ethics of those involved in recruiting is really getting to be pretty bad. When you go to coaches' meetings now, what's the major topic? Ethics. How many coaches associations have developed codes of ethics? The only thing we can do is look at ourselves in the mirror and know that we're doing things the way that they should be done. If that means one less win or not signing that prospect, then I guess that's what we have to do. If you need to use negative recruiting as the edge to sign a prospect, then you need to look at what else you need to be doing for your program so that you don't have to resort to that kind of thing.

If You Can't Say Something Nice...

It's easy to do a lot of things on the phone than if you're one on one with a student. With a phone call, it's easier to deny everything that you just said. But what happens when the coach you've been badmouthing calls your athletic director to talk about some of the things that you were saying about their program?

We need to remember that, yeah, it's a tough, cruel world out there. I don't always get who I want. I don't always get who I need. But I give it my best effort. Are the players in your program right now the players that you want? Are they the players that you need and are they making the right decisions?

The bottom line in recruiting right now is that the student needs to be making decisions for themselves. Right now there's so many other people who are influencing these student-athletes that sometimes your recruits are just pulled in by these people.

I think we need to ask our recruits, "If you came to this campus and something happened that you could not play, would you still be happy on this campus?"

I think we get a lot of people that are out there that are going to these programs or settling for second best when they could have gone somewhere else that would have been a better fit for them, but they were influenced by factors that we have no control over.

Phone recruiting can be an effective tool to recruit student-athletes into your program. Remember, you don't have to be the one making all the calls. You can have your staff, faculty, student-athletes, alumni, financial aid, and admissions departments assist you in the telephone contact process.

Develop a personal style and use it consistently. Be prepared before you call and take notes as you talk. Use those notes as a jumping off point or conversation starter the next time you talk to the prospect. And most importantly, remember not to sink into negative recruiting when you are making telephone contacts. Telephone contacts can be a time-effective and cost-effective way to recruit players into your program.

Author Profile: Sheilah Lingenfelter

Sheilah Lingenfelter is the head softball coach at Ashland College. She is a 15-year veteran of recruiting wars in Divisions II and III. A national coach-of-the-year winner, she built Wittenberg University into a national power. Her teams are frequent visitors to the NCAA Division III softball tournament. Sheilah has served as chair of the NCAA Division III Softball Committee and is a member of the National Softball Coaches Association board of directors.

GV350.3
TC1

TO DEAL WITH
VE RECRUITING

by Pat Murphy

, for three years in a row, we made it to the final
ear we were the runner up and I had to watch the
the College World Series. I was getting a little tired
kept thinking to myself, "Maybe I'm spending too
hough time coaching that final game." In recruiting,
essing.

h is not something I particularly like to talk about —
 we face it an awful lot. I think it's something, since
 III and battled my way to a high level of recruiting,
e. If you can recruit for Claremont- Mudd-Scripps,

hen I worked for Notre Dame that it must really be
 be honest with you, the name Notre Dame opened a
d been in the top 20 for the last five years, and we had
ose three years. It's very difficult, however, because
 southern teams and also by nice weather. We didn't
olarships at Notre Dame when I was there. This added
. We also required an 1100-plus score on the SAT to
 didn't have any financial aid except for the top one
. Keep in mind that one percent of the incoming class
ng 1300, 1400, or 1500 on the SAT. I don't know what
 y opinion it's tough to sign a great player with that

acles. There's no question about it. Recruiting for Notre
recruiting job I've ever had. I've recruited for Claremont
iversity, and for Maryville College. I firmly believe that
 recruit at those institutions — small colleges that don't
ognition or some that have names that take you 20 min-
it for anybody.
re sometimes foolish to believe that major college foot-
w what they're doing all the time. If you've been around
, you realize the jobs done in the smaller colleges, with
r in some cases, revenue sports — is more difficult. We
 that they have. We don't have the recruiting services.
dating us with interest in playing for us. We're not se-

lecting. We're going out and recruiting. We're going out to seek and find, find and seek, and get them to sign. It's difficult.

When you think about negative recruiting, you're going to have to realize that we probably don't face half as much as they (football recruiters) do, because they're at a "dog-eat-dog" level a little more than maybe the rest of us. But, nonetheless, it happens. I faced it a lot when I was at Notre Dame. Notre Dame is an easy target. Sometimes Notre Dame people seemed to walk around with a little halo over their heads. Really, we were just another school in the Midwest trying to do the best we could. I believe it's a great institution and they turn out great people, but sometimes we got a "holier than thou" attitude and became a target.

A Notre Dame student-athlete is a little different than some other athletes. I know of schools that when kids are involved in a hit-and-run car accident, the news story appears on page three. If a Notre Dame student stole toilet paper out of the dormitory, the story ran on page one. We were targeted a little more than some other schools.

Negative Recruiting Is Everywhere

> "Negative recruiting has never kept me from signing a player."

Negative recruiting is human nature. It's part of all of us. At some time in your life, you may either be susceptible to saying something negative about someone else, or you'll pass along something that is rumored or what you assume is true. Negative recruiting is alive and well. It's happening today. We need to accept that.

The first thing I think about negative recruiting is that you just need to accept it, and don't worry about it. It's not going to make or break your recruiting class. Some would say, "What if someone down the street at a local college, recruiting head to head with you for some student-athlete, is engaging in negative recruiting? Would you still say, 'Don't worry about it?'" I'm telling you, in all my years of recruiting, negative recruiting never once kept me from getting a player. I've lost a prospect because of it, but I don't think I would have signed him anyway.

Players don't let negative recruiting become involved in the decision-making process. They have character. Trust them. People who unconsciously negatively recruit just don't have the self-control to not say something negative. There are negative aspects to any program. There are things you can come up with to be negative about any school. Any student-athlete who is interested in going to a place where everything is perfect is dreaming, because there's something negative about every school.

When I hear that some other coach has said something negative about our program, I don't try to dispel the story, if it's true. I just try to answer to it as a matter of fact. If someone says to me, "Hey, so-and-so told me that four kids transferred from here last year." I say, "Yeah, they sure did." Try to just move right on. I don't want to get into a shouting match. I don't want to let that student-athlete see me sweat about it. If they want to know about it, I'll tell them all about it. I have nothing to hide. I don't try to keep anything from anybody, except if somebody wants to talk about my personal life — then they might be stepping across the boundary. I'd prefer not to discuss my personal life, but if you'd like to know about it, I'll tell you. When you're talking about your program, don't ever let them see you sweat; just move on.

How To Combat Negative Recruiting

There are methods of going back and attacking a negative recruiting situation without letting the student-athlete know it even bothered you. I never belittle myself and go for the "eye-for-an-eye" type of situation. I'm not going to let that happen. If they're talking bad about the school I'm coaching at, if they're talking bad about the weather, the schedule, or whatever it may be, I let them do that. A smart student-athlete out there that you are recruiting is going to realize that the coach didn't even defend himself. He talked honestly and openly about the situation, but didn't jump on it in a defensive mode. When the time came up to discuss a sensitive issue, I want them to remember that I addressed it completely.

> **"Be up-front and honest with each and every player you are recruiting."**

At the same time I want them to remember that I covered any accusation or concern that they had. I may even admit to it. "Yeah, one kid transferred last year. He's a third round draft pick. He was unhappy." I tell them what happened. I tell them that he didn't get the playing time he wanted. Then I tell the prospect, "I told him what I'm telling you — if you come here and playing time is of vital importance, I can't guarantee you it." I tell that to any recruit.

I think we sometimes feel in recruiting that we have to present a perfect scenario for a prospect, but I don't think that's the case. I think we need to be direct and tell prospects the truth. We need to lay all of the cards on the table. Remember, if negative recruiting is going to be important to a prospect, that student is only a prospect and not a player. There's no prospect in the world who becomes your player because of something negative he heard about somebody else. It doesn't happen.

Some coaches hit below the belt, there's no question about that. But student-athletes are smart enough to recognize it. They know about the bad and the good. And I think it's important that we don't get defensive, and not lower ourselves.

Issue-Oriented Negative Recruiting

I'll tell you a funny story that happened while I was at Notre Dame. Notre Dame was involved in recruiting a football/baseball player, one of the top players in the country. This student was on the cover of Sports Illustrated. It was a big deal. I was involved for about two years with this student because he was a fairly good baseball player. So we were recruiting back and forth and flying in for home visits. I'm getting a chance to watch Lou Holtz do his thing. The guy's a master at it.

One of the things that comes up in talking with him is that this young man thought that Notre Dame's social life wasn't very good. It was my turn to call the young man. I call him and we talk for a while, and pretty soon, the subject of Notre Dame's social life comes up. I asked him, "Are you concerned about the social life?"

He said, "Well, coach, I heard about it from [another coach] so-and-so."

First of all, never address the other coach. Sometimes other coaches will put down your school when talking to a prospect. Here's what I told him, "You're playing two sports. You're going to be going through a pretty good academic institution. You're going to be very busy. I think you'll make your own social life. Whatever it is you want to do, you'll probably be able to do it in that allotment of time."

> **"If you can't offer a prospect what he or she wants in a program, don't badmouth the program that does."**

But if social life to this prospect is being in a big city, or being around whatever, if you can't offer it, you can't offer it. You have to work with what you have, and be honest.

Well, the football recruiters got a little panicked. Instead of looking at it as, "Hey, you don't want to come here because the social life isn't good," and thinking we got the wrong kid, they were looking at it in terms of, "Hey, this kid's a superstar. We need him."

Now the student is ready to make his official visit, right at the end, before the signing period. You know what the recruiters were thinking: Let's have some social life. So they set the recruit up with a Notre Dame student who they thought would be pretty social. Believe me, he's very social.

Saturday morning rolls around and it's time for Coach Murphy to take over. So I meet him for their early morning football practice. I meet the recruit Saturday morning just before football practice. He was ghostly white. He was Caucasian but his skin was looking very, very, very white. I'm looking at him and realizing he's so hung over that his mouth is parched and he can hardly separate his lips to talk to me.

I had all of these things set up for him. I had a football/baseball player from our program lined up who was going to speak to him. I had a meeting with an alumni director who was a former baseball player who has a lot of insight into both football and baseball. And I was thinking, this kid won't be able to speak to him, he had such a miserable hangover.

This kid had the worst visit in the world. What he perceived as a social life and what our coaches perceived as a social life were two completely different things. After the visit, the recruit went home and decided on another school. Then he blamed Notre Dame, saying Notre Dame was a crazy place, a party place.

It just goes to show you that we try to sometimes overcompensate for certain negative (or perceived negative) aspects of our schools. A school in a small town may not be as exciting as one in a place like Miami or Los Angeles, but you just have to accept that. Focus on your program's strengths.

I think we as coaches spend a lot of time catering to some of our recruits. I think that's where we're going wrong in recruiting. I have some strong opinions about this topic. One of the things I've been lucky about is that people tend to associate me with success. I don't think I'm all that successful as a coach, to be honest with you, but I've been lucky to get good jobs and be in good situations. But I have to remind myself to be real. I'm not going to fall into the trap that I see so many of my friends falling into — trying to be something you're not. It happens a lot in college football and basketball. It hurts me to see it happen. I think sometimes we think if we're not in those sports, we think that they have some secrets or magic recruiting tricks.

Creating a Relationship with Recruits

During my time at Notre Dame, I learned a lot from Lou Holtz. He's a good recruiter and he has recruiting secrets for us. Holtz knows human nature. He knows people. And recruiting for him is not about sales. Recruiting for him is a relationship. It's a match. It's not about winning or losing a recruit. No, if he loses a recruit, they stop and evaluate what they did or didn't do in the recruiting process.

Consistency Is One Key to Success

Usually we could tell what we didn't do right. We'd look at our performance and say we were sporadic or we didn't inform the recruit from day one to the final day. We called the recruit in July and then we called him again in September. And then we decided we wanted him. We weren't sure at first. We weren't consistent. So often we want to spill our guts the first time we talk to a prospect — you can make a great contribution to our team, you can do this, you can do that. Then three weeks later, well, maybe not. Then four weeks later, yeah, maybe you can. And the recruit, meanwhile, is on a roller coaster.

I don't think we need to spell out to the recruit what he or she is going to do for

> **"Competition is not a win/lose proposition. You can't sign every player."**

our program. I think what we need to do is be straight with them from the start. Tell them, I want to see if our school is for you. I'd love to have you come in here. We'd love to have you as part of our program, *as of right now*. Let's see if it fits. Let's keep working at it. Let's build a personal relationship. Then if you say no, I'll see you down the road. We'll compete against each other. We'll shake hands after the game, and I'll say, "How're you doing, Mark? It's good to see you. You're doing a great job."

The truth of the matter is, I think we get into the competitiveness. It's competitive, but it's not a win/lose situation. We look at 60 recruits. We want a home visit from 25. We bring in 20 to visit us. Of that 20, we want to sign six.

We're going to lose some. I tell them that up front. We bring them in for recruiting visits and make it really nice for them. But I also tell them, I'm not sure who's going to come here and who's not. I'm going to tell you right now, we don't need any of you, but I hope that you come here anyway or I wouldn't be sitting here.

What kills me is that people think that great recruits are what make great coaches. That's what they think. Great players may make coaches look better. But great players aren't great recruits. Recruits are prospects. They have potential. Usually, great players develop because of great leaders. Great leaders enable those players to achieve to their highest potential. Great players are helped along by great leaders and great coaches. Then they can maximize their potential. They are no longer recruits.

Playing the Odds

In this recruiting thing, who are we kidding? In football, they sign the 30 best prospects each year. I see 8 to 10 of them who end up never playing. And they still have their high school clippings about how great a prospect they were — a future Hall of Famer or some such thing. It's only a projection.

There's no way you can project every kid correctly. But sometimes, there are clues. In football, it's pretty safe to say that a 5'11", 180 pound player is not going to play as a college offensive guard. But in sports such as baseball, we don't have that luxury.

It's tough to see what's inside a prospect, but one of the ways to find out what a person is made of is to see how he or she reacts to negative recruiting, and see how a prospect reacts to the way you treat him.

When our prospects came to Notre Dame, they stayed in the dorms. That's low budget baseball. I could have afforded to put them in the nicest hotel in town and I could have had ice sculptures, but that wouldn't have shown them what the university was like.

Some colleges fix them a beautiful meal: thin-sliced venison, lamb and roast beef. Some of the prospects didn't even know what it was. They had no idea what they were eating. It's ridiculous what some colleges set up for them. It's almost unbelievable.

I remember walking around Notre Dame with a football/baseball recruit. They set up the football locker room with all the old jerseys in there, from George Gipp to Paul Hornung to Johnny Lujack. All former Heisman Trophy winners.

In baseball, we put them in the dorms. You know what they had to eat? They ate with our players in the cafeteria, because that's what you're going to get when you come to our school. Show the prospect what it's going to be like when he comes on campus.

When a prospect comes to the campus, they might say, "Hey, they didn't take us anywhere. But when I went to Miami, we went on a cruise, we met these people, and went to five parties." Even if the prospect likes to do that type of thing, you don't want to show him or her that. I prefer to say, "What you see is what you get." I don't even dress up. I say, "Hey, this is the way I dress."

> **"One of the best things you have to offer a player is an environment that meets his needs."**

If a prospect is going to pick the university because I am wearing a nice tie, then I don't think I want that player. It's not a matter of not respecting a prospect, it's rather a matter of being yourself. When people take shots at me, it's because I'm vocal and because I say what I feel. People will say that I'm too tough to play for, or that I'm a maniac. They say, "You don't want to play for him." I say to the recruit, "Hey, maybe you don't. Check it out. Find out. Talk to the players."

Trust Your Recruits To Do Their Homework About Your School

Prospects are not stupid. If the player's worth having, he or she is going to do the research. They're not going to worry about negative stuff. They may say, "I heard your athletic department's in trouble." I tell them to find out. Go to people who know. I don't need to address that stuff.

I want to build a relationship with a prospect and a prospect's family that will let him know that I'm going to be consistent all the way through. If, in fact, it doesn't work out at the end, then it doesn't work out. It wasn't a match. Do I get disappointed when I lose a recruit? Yeah. I get disappointed. But it won't make or break my program.

Recruiting Is Vital

We're going to work our tails off in recruiting. Don't let me leave you with the impression that recruiting isn't vital. It is vital. But not more important than coaching. It's not more important than the discipline of the program. It's not more important than the way the program is consistently operated. But it is a vital piece of the pie. I work my tail off every year. I'm doing it today and 365 days a year.

In college baseball it's very different because we have the draft to contend with. I once signed six players in the early signing period. Three of them were drafted. That really bothers me. I worked my tail off from July 1 after a player's junior year and now I have to re-recruit him, because some guy with a Major League club saw him and said, "Wow, that gun registered 86 mph, let's sign him."

> **"Make no mistake about it. Recruiting is a vital activity for every program."**

College baseball recruiting isn't easy. At the same time, I don't think we need to prostitute ourselves for these players. They're doing it in football and basketball and in my opinion, that's where the problems are right now. They're kissing you-know-what, in order to get a player to come and then they have to live with the problems that causes for four years. One player may be a step faster, but that isn't the difference. Who are we kidding? I know in smaller colleges, there's a thing called "team concept" that we all don't want to talk about, because it's kind of corny. But the team concept is what it's all about. You'll find if you recruit one person one way and another person another way, you don't have the team concept.

Who do you need to be recruiting just as much as a scholarship player? The walk-ons. I learned that from my Division III experience. Recruit a walk-on as if they're the greatest player. They're an important part of the program.

Recruiting Mistakes

We all make mistakes in recruiting; I've made them myself. I've recruited a person who I thought was going to be a good player, who turned out to be horrible. And I admit it. We all should admit it, because we do. We spend three years trying to defend certain recruits — "This person can't play" or "He's got a horrible attitude" or "He doesn't work hard." We have to admit we made a mistake once in a while in recruiting. Say, "I made a mistake. Let's make the best of it."

Another mistake that schools sometimes make is in giving partial scholarships. We give a player a $10,000 partial scholarship and we immediately think that person has to perform to the *level* of $10,000. Wrong. That person's a member of your team. Forget the dollar amounts. Forget who is on scholarship. I know it's a tough thing to do because of the expectation that comes with giving a person $10,000.

That's too tough. A player lives with that expectation. They'll say, "Coach, you told me to come here. You're the one that offered me $10,000."

Coaches are at fault, too. I think we sometimes coach to that level. I think that's where we make a mistake. You show me a football coach who is secure enough to treat every recruit the same, and I'll show you a good program.

As for negative recruiting, don't lower yourself. It's human nature to want to defend yourself, but don't. Don't address it. Don't defend it. Don't attack it. Don't let it un-nerve you. Don't get irritated. Don't let it change your feelings about a prospect. The student-athlete will be smart enough to figure it out for himself or herself. You can then turn the negative into a positive by stressing good points about your program. The person who is using negative recruiting against you obviously doesn't have enough positives in their own program. But you can stress good points in your own program that can maybe even demonstrate weaknesses in someone else's program.

> **"Emphasize the positive in your program rather than the negative in someone else's."**

Develop Your Own Recruiting Style

Know your strengths. You have your own recruiting system, the different ways you like to recruit. I know some women volleyball coaches who are just incredible recruiters. I wish I could recruit the way that they can. I can't. They're just themselves. This one particular coach I'm thinking of is the greatest recruiter in the world because she's just herself. There is nothing fancy about her system.

You do need to be organized. You have to work your tail off and stay consistent with the recruits. You can't recruit them for a while and then drop them. There's nothing wrong with making a phone call and saying, "Hey, Sally, we've decided that we're not going to offer you a scholarship." You're doing that recruit a favor. That's being first class.

Don't be afraid to tell the truth. Don't be afraid to go right at it. Be a good person. Have character. Some say that we shouldn't talk about that kind of stuff. I say, "That's what it's all about. You've set up your own system, your own way. Be comfortable with it and make sure your assistants are comfortable with it."

Work your tail off. Be direct and straight. You don't want to spend your time talking about another program. You have enough to tell them about your own program or about yourself. Or talk about them. Everybody likes to talk about themselves. Get the prospects talking.

One of my assistants came to me one time and asked, "I've talked to this kid for five straight weeks now. What do I say,?" I tell them to ask the recruit a question. Ask, "How are you feeling? What are you thinking about college? Are there things about our school that you want to talk about?"

This "recruiting thing" is overrated when it comes to signing the top prospect. You should go out and spend more time finding out what's inside the recruit. You find out more about what they're going to develop into by finding out what's inside of them now. If you do that, you'll be successful.

Life Savers Theory

I heard somebody describe it like this: We all get a pack of Life Savers. What do we do? We all go to the red ones. Be honest with me. No one goes for the yellow ones. The orange one, maybe, is a second choice. The green one, no way. You leave that in the pack. Then you throw it out. Everybody wants the red Life Saver.

> **"Keep an open mind to all the possibilities."**

But you know what, if you just get orange Life Savers, and you start eating them, they're pretty good. You spend all your time digging through the pack to get the red Life Saver and the orange one is sometimes just as good. The lesson is — we can all be mesmerized with what a certain prospect can mean to our program, but we need to keep an open mind to other possibilities. Orange lifesavers are good, too.

Hallmarks of Great Recruiters

The greatest recruiters that I know on the road sit by themselves, watching, listening, and not making comments. How do you know when recruiters don't know what the heck they're doing? On the road, they stand next to you. They say, "Hey, how you doing? What do you think of Joe? Think he can run?"

I know this coach doesn't know what he's doing. Then I like to have some fun with him. One time, a good friend and I were recruiting a player from Ohio, Chad Green. He could really run. We were watching him one day — the coaches from Georgia Tech, Clemson, Miami, and myself. We're all sitting together; we're all pretty good friends. Sure enough, this player comes up to hit. The other coaches didn't really know about him, but I'd been there a few more days than they had. I know they're going to write down his name when the announcer says it. So I talk real loud right as he says the player's name, so they don't hear it. Then the player gets up and hits a ground ball to short and he flies to first. We've all got our stopwatches going. Whoa — 4.1.

"Wow," they asked, "who is that kid?" I turned to my buddy, and I said, "Jack, his name is Rudy Adeer." He asked me, "How do you spell that?" I spelled it for him — Rudy Adeer." "Really?" he asked. "How did you know about him?" I said I'd known about him for a long time. I said he'd been to our camp and I went on and on.

Jack asked me if he was a good student. I indicated he was a good student, a good player. I told my buddy he couldn't get in Notre Dame, and that he was looking to go down south. Then I said, "I have his phone number right here." I gave him my phone number. After that I went on and on for about 20 minutes. All three coaches listened to me. Two nights later, I was at home. I got three calls for Rudy Adeer.

Sometimes I think that we take recruiting far too seriously. I think we don't stop to realize what we're doing. And sometimes I think we believe that these student athletes aren't as smart as they really are. But they are. They know what's going on. They're listening. If you put yourself in their shoes, they know what's going on. They know who really cares about them. They know who's really interested.

When Negative Recruiting Happens at the Prospect's High School

Honesty is important, especially if you haven't called a prospect in a while. You won't lose if you call and say, "Hey, we haven't called you in four months because to be honest with you, we were recruiting three other guys. We found out that those three other guys don't fit us. We now want to recruit you. I know we're late and I hope you don't hold that against us. I hope that you give us a chance to prove to you that we earnestly do want you. We might not have at the beginning or we might not have seen it as clearly or we might not have thought we had a good chance with you, but now we do and we'd like to take that chance."

There's another issue to consider, and that's the high school coach who's ticked off because his player or her player came to your school and didn't have a good experience. The student may have left or didn't play or was "promised a big start." This becomes the negative recruiting. A high school coach may say to the player, "Hey, you don't want to go to Central Iowa. Too many players have had bad experiences there."

> **"Beware of the high school coach who holds a grudge."**

How does a coach deal with that? How do you deal with a high school coach who just doesn't like you because you're 35 and they're 61? They're ticked off that they aren't where you are in their careers or they think you're cocky or they went to a different school. How do you deal with it?

For the most part, in my opinion, the high school coach isn't the key in recruiting anyway. But I think if you feel he or she is a strong enough factor in the decision, then you go to the coach and say, "Hey, look. Here's our situation. I have reason to believe that you don't think it's a good decision for Johnny or Joanie to come to our school. Let's talk about that."

Once again, be honest. Be direct. Whether or not it turns out well, that coach knows what you're saying. That coach realizes that they probably should not have made negative comments. There are some high school coaches out there who hate me, because I don't go through them to get to the player. I don't want their opinions about whether their kid can play or not. Don't get me wrong — I do value their opinions. But I don't base everything on their opinions. I think they have some great knowledge to share with us. I think the high school coaches can tell us

Q&A

Question: *If you've recruited student athletes and then they turn you down, do you try to find out why? I'd like to know what they did not like about my program but they're not willing to tell me.*

Answer: I think that's a good thing to know. I'm my own worst critic. I'm hard on myself and I want to know. I ask the kids real strong questions. But it's knowing *when* to ask that is the key. I'll tell you when to ask them – when it's over. That's the toughest phone call for them to make. You've been in a house when the prospect says, "Well, the one thing that scares me is what I'm going to tell the coach at the University of Illinois — that I'm not going there." That's a scary phone call for that young person to make. They don't want to make that phone call. It's tough. Mom and Dad keep saying, "You've got to call that coach."

So when they are talking to you to tell you no, I try to make them feel comfortable. I say, "Hey, don't worry about it. You made the choice to go to UCLA — congratulations! Super! You guys will get along; it's going to be great, I hope that you have four great years there. That's a super decision."

I don't want to keep them on the phone because the prospect doesn't want to be on the phone with me. I don't want to make him feel uncomfortable because you know what, that comes back to help you in recruiting. If you ask him "Right now, what was the reason, right now," he's thinking, "I can't tell him that I thought he was a jerk." They usually won't do that. They would say something kind of soft. "Well, I had kind of a better feel for the place." Really what they're saying is "Hey, when I went out that night with the guy on your team, he got me drunk and I don't drink," or whatever it may be.

So I don't think that is an appropriate time to ask. I think you can ask the recruiting host because I put a lot of pressure on the recruiting host to talk. I tell them "I'm choosing you to represent our program." I have a meeting with all the recruiting hosts before the prospects come in and those recruiting hosts get background information and a sense of how we feel about a recruit. And I use information from the recruiting host about what the player did or didn't like.

I don't think we ever can really know why a person said no, and I think there is a time, later on, maybe when you run into that person, or when that person's a sophomore at the other school that you can get bits and pieces.

a lot about prospects. But we need to listen to everything. We should also ask them questions about a prospect, outside of just sport skills. You don't have to ask them, "Can Joey run?" I can see that for myself. Can Joey hit? I can see that for myself. Ask them other questions. Ask about Joey's family, about how Joey reacts to situations. "Has Joey ever been in this situation? Has Joey ever sat on the bench for you? How did Joey react then?" Ask some other people. That's when you should ask assistant coaches and fellow players.

Recruiting is about seeking, finding, matching up, building relationships, acting consistently, and then letting the prospect make the choice. The recruit is the one who makes the choice.

When you pull your guns out and start shooting, you're desperate. That's why people get fired. That's why people get frustrated. Trust your prospects to do the right thing.

I don't want to say anything negative about other coaches. You would not believe the number of players who come back to me and say, "You know, coach, I really appreciate that you didn't take a shot at Coach so-and-so. All he did was talk about how bad you guys were. He never talked about his program."

The other thing is, don't let some 18- or 19-year-old dictate how you're going to recruit. If that 18- or 19-year-old comes back and says, "I really didn't like how you guys didn't pick me up at the airport. I really didn't like how you guys put me in that sleazy hotel." You got to take it with a grain of salt. You can't let them evaluate your way of doing things.

You'll be successful if you work hard at it and you're honest and you're organized, and you care about them and you build a relationship, and you don't get mad at the player who chooses someplace else. Find someone else. There's a lot of Life Savers in the package. If you work hard enough, those green ones don't taste all that bad. That's the truth.

Author Profile: Pat Murphy

Pat Murphy is the head baseball coach at Arizona State University. Pat's resume includes 17 years of college recruiting experience on the Division I and Division II levels. A recipient of several coaching awards, Pat's other coaching stops include Maryville College, Claremont-Mudd-Scripps College, Florida Atlantic University and the University of Notre Dame.

ORGANIZING HOME AND CAMPUS VISITS

by Debbie Ryan

I want to tell you a story about a prospect I signed — one of the top 10 prospects in the country — with whom I never had a home visit. Her name was Dena Evans. We started recruiting Dena in her junior year. Dena was a point guard from Texas and we tried to get her to consider us. She was a Rhodes Scholar-type — an excellent student.

Dena said, "I'm really not interested in Virginia; I've narrowed my schools down to three, so you're going to need to move on to somebody else." So I did. I ended up recruiting Molly Goodenbauer who, as many of you know if you follow women's basketball, played at Stanford and had a very successful career there.

We came down to the wire with Molly. The day that Molly decided to go to Stanford, a door was opened for me that I didn't even know was going to open. The interesting thing about this was that Dena Evans wanted to go to another school, but that school evidently did not have a position for her and did not really need her. They were looking at bigger point guards. Dena was a small point guard, and this particular school did not want a small point guard.

Dena's second choice was Stanford. The day she called Stanford, Molly Goodenbauer had already called Stanford to say she was coming. So, that took away Dena's opportunity at Stanford. Now, Dena was down to one school and it was really not where she wanted to go. I had a former player who was working at the University of Texas. My former player called me in the middle of the recruiting period, and asked, "Do you want Dena Evans?" And I said, "Do I want Dena Evans? I just got turned down by Molly Goodenbauer. I wanted Dena a year ago, but she wasn't interested in us." She said, "If you want Dena Evans, you can get her. You can get her by the end of the weekend!"

So I called Dena Evans on Friday night. She was about to head out to a football game. I talked to her for maybe two or three minutes, because she was on her way to the game and was more interested in that than talking to me. But we did set up a time for her to make an official visit.

There's an unusual rule regarding prospects from Texas — if Texas schools have started their season, a prospect cannot make an official visit to a university and have it paid for. Her school had already started practice; this was in November. So Dena could not visit Virginia without paying for it herself.

It turned out she was allowed to come for a visit at Virginia, pay for the visit herself, and then we were allowed to reimburse her after her season was over. That was the way the rule was implemented.

Dena and her dad came for a 12-hour visit. It wasn't a very long visit; because coming from Texas, she lost an hour with the time zone change. She came on Tuesday; the next day was the end of the signing period. So I had to send her a letter of intent by Federal Express and she had to sign it before she left home — not knowing whether she even liked Virginia or not.

She signed it, because by the time they got back home, she wouldn't have been able to sign; the signing period would have been over. Dena and her dad both signed the letter, got on the plane, and came to Virginia.

Dena spent maybe eight hours on the grounds. We took her all around and we visited with her a little bit. The only thing she knew about me and about our program was what her high school coaches had told her.

We went to dinner that night and Dena seemed like she was having a pretty good time. But we really didn't spend a lot of time together. The next morning they had to get up at 5:00 a.m. to catch a 6:00 a.m. plane back to Texas. We got Dena and her dad to the airport and I asked, "Well, did you like the visit?" She said, "Yeah, I really liked the visit. I've decided to come to Virginia."

Why Prospects Choose Your School

Recruiting is really strange, isn't it? Do prospects choose an institution because of your athletic program, your particular sport, or the way that your school treats that athletic sport? Do prospects choose the program because of the school and the academic reputation and the atmosphere of the school? Do prospects choose a program because of the coach?

> **"Many decisions are made based on emotions, not fact."**

I would say that a lot of recruits end up making their decisions based on the coaching staff and who they're going to be with during the four years that they're there. That's why I think a lot of prospects, when they do make errors, make them because they choose a school that really doesn't fit them. They don't go through the process properly. Instead, they make an emotional decision. They decide on a coach. Then they get there and all of a sudden, they find out that their major isn't offered; they don't have this; they don't have that. They're all confused, because they weren't even listening during the recruiting process.

The Home Visit

I'm a very laid back recruiter. And that's an amazing thing, because there aren't many things in life that I'm laid back about. I think it's because I'm not particularly comfortable in huge social settings. So I do very well when I take a laid back approach. I try to tailor the whole recruiting process around the prospect that we're recruiting.

For instance, the recruitment of one of my players, Tammi Reiss, was very different from the recruitment of Dawn Staley, another player. Tammi received many phone calls, just like Dawn did, but Tammi didn't enjoy talking on the phone at all. She had too many other things that she wanted to do. She was involved in four sports. She was involved in every school activity possible; she had no interest in talking on the phone.

Then there was Dawn, who only wanted to talk to people who didn't want to talk about basketball. I happened to be one of those people. I really got to know Dawn through telephone conversations — that was a neat experience. These two recruitments were very, very different. The two home visits were very different.

You need to be yourself. The other thing that's important is to tailor the whole recruitment process around the prospect, what the prospect likes, and what the prospect feels is important. One of the things that we do right away is to identify the coach who's going to be the most effective with the player.

When you go on a home visit, you want that assistant coach with you. When you walk into a home, the person who's been recruiting that player should be at that home visit with you. A lot of times before we even go on a home visit, we will double-team a player. We like to send an assistant coach. It's also very good for parents to be able to have an assistant coach in their home. You may have made specific contact with the parent, which is something that we do. But you don't have as much phone contact as you used to have. So having the assistant in the home with you is critical.

> **"Use your assistant coaches as part of the recruiting process."**

We start off early trying to find a date that's suitable for both the recruiters and the prospect. I know a lot of prospects are not interested in thinking about dates coming up on their calendars. We use mailings to remind them that it's coming. We might even send them a copy of the calendar for September and October just to remind them that they need to start filling it in and they need to start thinking about these things.

You need to start planning the home visit early. We always try to send somebody early, if not the day of the visit, maybe the day before. A lot of times, if an assistant and I are traveling together, it gives me a chance to be at home a little bit longer. She goes out early, spending time with the player and the family.

This is especially helpful when we recruit across the country. If we're recruiting in California, we use our contacts out there, one right after the other, and hit them with a double whammy right away.

My assistant will go out on a Monday, see the player at school, maybe have dinner with the family that night, get to know the family a little bit. Then I come in after that and do the home visit the next night. The two-day plan gives the prospect and the family a chance to see us in a different light.

We also try to utilize phone calls on the day of the home visit. If we're on the road, we always try to check in with the prospect's parents and make sure that the time we've scheduled is okay. We check with prospects and make sure that they're going to get home on time from whatever they're doing. Often there are adjustments that have to be made with families. We give them a courtesy call to confirm the time that we're going to meet.

We also believe it's important to follow-up with a phone call. You have unlimited phone calls on the day of the home visit, and we try to include a follow-up call. For instance, if you had a home visit on a Sunday afternoon, it's a good idea to follow-up that night with a call. Questions come up after you leave. A call is a good reminder that you were there and it keeps you "in the home" a little bit longer.

Dressing for Recruiting Success

When we visit a player's home, it's important to consider the way you dress. Many times we won't go into a home dressed "completely casual," but we do like to dress so that the family feels comfortable with us. I am not comfortable in a business suit, so I don't wear them. I'm much better off if I wear a skirt or even walking shorts. I prefer a casual look. I'm not going to walk into a home with a warm-up suit on, and I'm not going to walk into a home wearing jeans. Tailor your dress to the prospect and the family.

The Importance of Research

> "Be sure to do your homework before a recruiting visit."

Make sure that you research the home that you're going into. You should be ready for anything. One time I went to Georgia to visit a young woman whom I knew did not have a telephone. When I finally arrived at her home, I found a one-room place, with no indoor plumbing. There were nine people living there. This was a very unusual situation for me. I didn't research the home situation and neither did my assistant.

I learned through trial and error that you really have to research the homes you're visiting. Be sure that you're ready for anything. Be sure that you're flexible. Be sure that you can communicate with all kinds of people. You can't go in with a prepared speech. You can't go in with an outline and think that you're going to be able to hit them with it. That is not the way to make a home visit. It's not the way to make the parents feel comfortable with you, nor is it a way to make the prospect feel comfortable with you. It just shouldn't happen that way.

What I find effective is to figure out what works for each individual home, each individual family, each individual recruit, and the diversity that they may bring. It requires a lot of work. It's not just talking to one person in the family — the recruit — but it's talking to other people in the family. Whether it be brothers, sisters, or parents, you may have to tailor your home visit a lot differently than you normally would. There are going to be times when you are meeting with a family and you believe that they want you to stay longer; when, in truth, they are hoping you will leave. I don't know if you've ever been in that situation, but I've had others tell me that. I find it really interesting. They stayed too long, and the prospect said, "I'm not going there."

Can you imagine putting everything into a home visit and having a kid say, "She stayed too long; I'm not going there"?

The Importance of Honesty

I find it important that you are honest and up front. We all come from different types of institutions and you probably recruit against all different kinds of coaches. You probably recruit against people that are as negative as they can be and who make stuff up about you. I don't like that. I prefer to be very up front and honest.

I even bring up some of the negatives about our institution, so that at least recruits know I'm legitimate. Everything that comes out of my mouth is not a positive in terms of our school or the athletic program. I think you have to do that every once in a while. You must answer honestly when a prospect asks you a question. If they ask you if you offer a communications major and you don't, don't try to make something up. Just tell them the truth.

> "I let prospects know about the negatives aspects of our institution."

I'll tell you what, prospects really appreciate it when you tell them the truth. I don't think that a particular major is going to make all that much difference in the end. I know that about 90 percent of student-athletes don't know what they want to do anyway, even though they may say they do.

What to Take With You

In most cases, I walk in with a folder and that's about it. I send everything else ahead. I send the prospect a packet including all the information I want to have at the home visit. Then I walk in with the folder because it reminds them of who they are talking to tonight; many times, on consecutive nights, they forget who it is they're talking to. The folder contains some things that I refer to. Most of the time this is all I walk in with. That's it.

We start off talking about the school. I'm fortunate to be at a very nice school with a beautiful campus. We talk about its location. We talk about the size. It's really a nice size — 12,000 undergraduates and 18,000 total students. We also have a good professor-to-student ratio.

Your school's reputation is built on what your graduates have done since they graduated. To be honest with you, you can get a good education anywhere. So I don't try to oversell the school at all. I think the school sells itself once the player arrives there. We send recruits a book called *The University of Virginia*. I'm sure that every school has a similar book. It's really about all the things that go on at the school including a little bit of information about each major. This is just an informational book, with a lot of color in it, available to all students. It has pictures of the university and talks about social life, sororities, fraternities, all the different organizations.

Having The Right Information Handy Is the Key to Answering a Prospect's Questions

> **"Be prepared to answer almost any question a prospect might have."**

We make sure to bring the book about the university with us to the home visit because sometimes questions come up. One question that often comes up is the "student body" question — "What is the make-up of your student body?" A lot of times parents as well as student-athletes want to know what the composition of your school is. Having been there 20 years, I might be able to answer that question, but the information book can come in handy for such details.

We try to have as much information available as possible, in case they ask us a question we can't answer. For instance, you may be asked about crime at your school. You may be asked for exact statistics. That's a question I was asked one time during a home visit. So, I started carrying the information book with me — the crime issue is discussed in a section called "Safety and Security."

Our information book happens to be pretty comprehensive. For example, the "Safety and Security" section talks about security in the dorms and about the lighting throughout the university.

If you have them, bring information books or pamphlets published by your university; they are often helpful during home visits.

Academics & The Recruiting Process

We spend a great deal of time discussing the major that the student-athlete may be interested in. During the home visit, we also talk about graduation rates, something I'm very proud of. We have a very high graduation rate and we talk about that. One thing, I think, that is important about the academics at any school is the support system. We spend a lot of time explaining what the support system at our university is like.

We graduate a lot of student-athletes; our graduation rate is around 90% for student-athletes and it's 95% for the regular student body. When you have good graduation rates, it's obvious that your support system is fairly strong. Ours is a good university that supports its students — not just our athletes, but all students.

That is evident in the overall graduation rate. We talk about the fact that it's not just the student-athletes that receive good support, it's the entire student body.

We spend most of our time on the area of class scheduling. Recruits and their parents want to know if student-athletes get priority scheduling. That subject is a real stickler right now, and it's becoming a real negative for some schools, because they don't offer it. There are a lot of great schools that don't have priority scheduling. If your school doesn't have priority scheduling, emphasize that student-athletes get the courses that they need at the times they need without priority scheduling.

Another issue that comes up frequently is tutoring. Parents ask, "How often can my son or daughter be tutored?" We review all of this information with recruits and parents.

I require that our student-athletes go to study hall three times a week during their first year. Then I don't require it, as long as they're not in any academic trouble. If they're in academic trouble, they are required to attend study hall.

What about class attendance in relation to travel? How do you travel? Do student-athletes miss a lot of class because you take the bus all the time or because you drive vans? These are questions we hear a lot during home visits. You have to give honest answers. If students miss 10 days of the semester, you should tell them, "We miss 10 days of each semester."

If you take an academic advisor or tutor on the road to help with studies, you need to let them know that, too. Emphasize how you plan to help students keep up with their studies.

Parents sometimes ask if the coaches are involved in the player's academic development. In other words, if a student-athlete is not attending study hall, what are the consequences? That's a good question.

For me, if a student-athlete is not attending study hall, he or she does not play.

They come and sit at practice and they watch. If they do it twice, they don't play in the next game. If they do it a third time, I say, "See ya."

It's just not worth it. If you make an appointment with someone, you need to be responsible to be there.

Prospects should know exactly how you're going to handle them and exactly how you're going to discipline them. That's important.

Selling the Benefits of Your School's Career Development Program

We spend some time visiting about career development and job opportunities. We also include summer job opportunities. We have a network of people in our career planning and placement office that do a nice job both with summer jobs and with career jobs.

You can really emphasize that, especially if you have a successful network in your area or across the country. If you have a good career planning and placement department, it's good to bring that up. One item we bring along to the home visit is information about internships. You may not realize it, but most of your schools offer these. Internships are important to career development, so we talk a little bit about that.

About Summer School...

We also spend time discussing summer school. In our situation, student athletes are allowed to attend as much summer school as they want under NCAA regulations, which is nine hours. Our kids can have all nine hours if they want it. Not every sport at Virginia has that luxury; but as the women's basketball team, we do and it's all paid for.

There are other things you need to let recruits and parents know. They may ask, "How many sessions of summer school do you have? How long is summer school? Do you have four-week sessions? Do you have eight-week sessions? How exactly does it work?"

Parents want to know how long their kids will be home during the summer. We really need to let them know whether or not

Q&A

Question:

What if you are visiting a recruit who isn't very interested in academics? Do you start with basketball and put the academics second? Do you make basketball bigger and talk about your athletic program more so?

Answer:

I have never started a conversation by talking about basketball in my entire career. I think that is primarily because I'm at an institution where, if you're not a little bit interested in academics, you can't make it.

There have been times when I've gone pretty quickly through the academic situation though.

We try to screen prospects, to a certain degree, academically. We have been known to take at-risk students. But we've done very well with the graduation rate, so I think we've been allowed a little bit of luxury and flexibility.

Now, I know if they'll make it, just by looking at their transcripts.

summer school is going to be important. Then we move on to talking about dorms and dining. We talk a little bit about the school itself and the dorms and the dining facility. You'd be surprised how interested kids are in the dining situation.

I do spend some time talking about the prospect. I talk a lot about how she fits our needs in the program, how I would work with her and help to develop her.

We may talk about her weaknesses and her strengths, and how I would take advantage of her strengths with our offense, and how I would help her with her weaknesses. I also try to make some prediction as to how much playing time she would get.

Prospects and the Question of Playing Time

I would never "promise" one minute of playing time. I don't promise them anything. I make that very clear. When a player says to me in their freshman year, "You promised..." I say, "Hey, I didn't promise one thing." Because I will not do that. I have people on my staff who played for me who say, "She didn't promise me anything, so I don't believe that she would promise you anything."

That's the good thing. You can't promise them anything. But I do try to make a calculated guess as to what a continuum of playing time would be. I can't say to recruits that they're not going to play at all and I can't say that they're going to play 40 minutes. But — if they're not going to play much in their freshman year, I really do try to let them know.

> **"Never promise anything you can't deliver."**

Recruits have a choice. They can go to a school where they're going to start and play a lot, or they can come here and work like everybody else did to get into the starting lineup to get their playing time.

Planning for the Future

One of the most frequent questions that I get is, "Are you going to be there for the rest of my career?" The way I handle that is to say, "I'm planning to be here, but if I were to walk across the street tomorrow and get hit by a bus, I can't control that." I get that question a lot, and I think primarily it's because sometimes it's used negatively by other coaches.

You may be sitting and talking casually to your colleagues. Maybe you had a bad year and you say something like, "I'm really thinking about going into administration or something." Then all of a sudden it's all over the place that you're leaving to be the athletic director at Wyoming State.

We've even had questions about assistant coaches, if they are going to stay. Players become very close to the coaching staff. Coaches have to be honest with student-athletes about what's going on.

We also spend some time on philosophy and style of play. We have a style of play that's typical. We run, we press, we play defense. We do have a little bit of an international style. I like to develop my post players to be able to play on the perimeter, and let them take three-point shots.

Tips for the Master Recruiter

> **"Emphasize how your program strengths can help the prospect."**

If you're going out to recruit a sprinter, don't tell prospects that you're the best long distance swimming coach in the country. Instead, talk about what his or her strengths are and how you're going to help develop those strengths. Discuss how your philosophy fits the athlete. You can't change your philosophy for a player, but you can sometimes guide a player who may not be exactly what you were looking for.

I also emphasize to prospects and their families that we have a lot of help at Virginia. We have a strength coach, a sport psychologist, and a nutritionist, along with an exercise physiologist. People sometimes ask me, "What do *you* do?" I've gotten pretty good at recruiting, because they send me on the road all the time. We talk about each one of those individuals and how they help our program.

Our nutritionist is very active with our players. Moms really appreciate that fact, especially with the female athletes. We are finding that our female athletes are starting to be affected by eating disorders. We don't even know they're ravaging their bodies. We really can't recognize it until sometimes it's almost too late. Our nutritionist spends a lot of time with each one of our athletes. I make a point of that.

Focus on the Individual

We also spend a lot of time on individual development. We like to talk about how that person is going to start out at one level and be at the next level four years later. One of the things that we're known for at Virginia is the fact that we do spend a lot of time on individual development.

Players want to know if they'll be able to take the next step. If I'm a world class swimmer or if I'm a lacrosse player, what are you developing me for? If there's indoor lacrosse or if there's a pro league in soccer for the men, they want to know their chances of moving on into that. We really build that part up. That's why we spend a lot of time on it.

Odds and Ends

We spend a little bit of time on the commitment required of the student-athlete. It's not a lot of time. You're going to have your pre-season conditioning; you're going to have your practice. Recruits are interested in how long that practice is going to be.

We talk some about our conference and the NCAA tournament. We spend a lot of time talking about television. We have a lot of television coverage and athletes want to know about that.

I include Olympic development in my home visits. I've coached for USA BASKETBALL and I spend some time talking about USA BASKETBALL and development in the Olympic system.

Then I spend some time on social life, but for me to tell recruits what the social life at Virginia is like would be a joke. They really need to come for a visit to find out what the social life is like.

We have some things that we always cover in a home visit. One of those is the honor system. We have a unique system at Virginia. Our institution was founded by Thomas Jefferson. It is completely student-run. There is not an ounce of adult supervision.

At Virginia, you can be thrown out for one violation of the honor code — lying, cheating or stealing. During the home visit, we explain how it works.

When we get to the end of our home visit, we usually show a highlight film. Some years our highlight films are really good.

You can produce a highlight film now that you can sell; but the highlight film that we are allowed to produce at this point is very generic.

We don't have a recruiting tape; we just show the highlight film at the end. Then we try to wrap it up and let them ask questions.

Campus Visits

For campus visits, we're very laid back. We don't bring our student-athletes into the gym and start playing tapes that have them winning the national championship. We don't take them in the locker room and have their jersey hanging there.

> **"Get your players involved in the recruiting during on-campus visits."**

We don't walk into a locker room where there are retired jerseys and pictures of retired people. We don't even put our student-athletes in hotels. Our players prefer that the recruits stay in their rooms with them. The players like recruits to stay on the campus. That's the way they want to do it.

I've asked them many times if this isn't an inconvenience, but they say, "No, we want them to stay here. It's much more fun this way, so they can find out what it's really like." We want them to see it just as it is. And I am just as I am everyday. We try not to do anything any differently.

I also don't try to make any one recruit more important than another. What I have found in recruiting women's basketball players, is that they don't like that. They don't like it when you single them out. I think they just want to see what it's like. They want to get a feeling. I guess they make a decision on something, whether it's the shoes you wear or the color of your uniform. I think they make a choice based on a feeling or a comfort level that they have. I think the more you make it like it's not going to be when the players are actually there, the harder it is.

We do have special events, like midnight madness. It is just a super weekend. We even had one player commit when she got off the airplane. She was so excited about the weekend, she committed right then and there. She said to me, "I'm coming here." I said, "The weekend's not even over yet!!"

> **"Tailor your visit to the prospect, but don't do anything out of the ordinary."**

Our campus visit is probably no different from what you do. One thing we don't do is have a lot of meetings. One thing I have learned from my student-athletes is that they don't want to go to a lot of meetings. So we try to stay away from one-on-one meetings that student-athletes seem to really be anxious about.

Instead, we bring the people we want the players to meet to the activity that we're having that day. For example, the academic advisor might come to a tailgate party or the nutritionist might come to dinner one night. They might not even talk to the student-athlete. If the parents are there, we'll let them entertain the parents. It gives the prospect an opportunity to get his or her questions answered without the formal structure of a series of meetings.

As I mentioned, we also have a strength coach, a sports psychologist and a nutritionist who work with our program. If we can, we also find a time to introduce these individuals to the recruits.

Make The Prospect Comfortable

One final note about the campus visit. We just really try to be accommodating and we show them what we have. We try to let them be comfortable. We let them spend as much time with the players as we can, because that's where they find out everything they really want to know anyway.

Focus on each individual recruit during the home and campus visits, make him or her comfortable with the process, and just let the prospect see what your program is all about. That's really all you can do.

Author Profile: Debbie Ryan

Debbie Ryan is the head women's basketball coach at the University of Virginia. A winner of National, District and Conference coach-of-the-year honors, her Cavalier teams have appeared in 14 consecutive NCAA tournaments and have been to the Final Four three times.

PSYCHOLOGICAL ASPECTS OF THE RECRUITING PROCESS

by Dan Smith

Many times when you think about a sport psychologist, it's easy to think "This guy's a shrink; what's he going to teach me as a coach?" When I coached, I would have thought that, too. I don't know what that guy is possibly going to do to help me in my coaching or help me be a better recruiter.

Actually, I started as a coach. I had absolutely no interest in ever going back for a Ph.D. in sport psychology when I left Brigham Young University with my undergraduate degree. I went back to the Los Angeles area where I grew up and I coached at a junior college there for two years. Then I was fortunate enough, at 23 years of age, to get the head basketball coaching job at Brigham Young University—Hawaii campus, an NAIA school. Besides that, the weather was pretty nice and there were a lot of nice things about living in Hawaii.

It was while I was in Hawaii as head coach that I learned how important the mental aspects of coaching were. If I had an athlete lacking in physical skill — maybe his shooting or ball handling wasn't up to par — the assistant coaches and I would work extensively with him on that physical skill. But if he were lacking in a psychological skill — such as being unable to shoot the ball in critical situations, having difficulty concentrating on the floor, not very goal-oriented, or if he was short tempered — we didn't quite know what to do. We'd think, "He either has it or he doesn't. If he doesn't have it, that's just tough luck. He doesn't make the team or I don't ever play him in critical situations."

I always thought that was unjust. We, as coaches, all realize that the mental aspect is important, and yet we turn right around and spend no time on mental training. At the time I was coaching, there was a guy named Dr. Rainer Martens at the University of Illinois who wrote a classic article in the field of sport psychology. He was the leading authority in the world in sport psychology. The title of the article was "From Smocks to Jocks."

I was quite interested in that article. He'd been the top laboratory researcher in the field of sport psychology for many years, but he didn't necessarily know if any of the issues he studied in the laboratory had any practical application in the real world of athletic competition. He wrote that it was time for laboratory "psychologists" to get out of the laboratory and get onto the playing field and see what worked and what didn't.So I decided I wanted to find out more about the field of sport psychology. I applied to the University of Illinois for their Ph.D. program with Rainer Martens. The head basketball coach from the University of Illinois, Lou

Henson, was also in Hawaii at that time, playing at the Rainbow Classic. I met with Lou to find out if there was a possibility that I could be assistant basketball coach on a part-time basis while I worked on a Ph.D. in sport psychology. He was interested and he seemed to think that would work out. I was fortunate enough to get accepted and I went to the University of Illinois for a Ph.D. in sport psychology.

During my third year on the basketball staff, I did my doctoral dissertation on an extensive psychological training program that I conducted with the basketball team at the University of Illinois. We were very fortunate — we were picked to finish sixth in the Big 10 that year, but ended up finishing second and had a really good year.

> **"Psychological training can be as important as physical training for your program."**

I was walking out to the car one day and our head football coach, Mike White (he was the head football coach of the Los Angeles Raiders at one time), was visiting with me. He said, "Boy, I've heard a lot about the psychological training program that you've used with the basketball team. Do you think next year you could conduct the same program with the football team?"

In basketball, you're dealing with 12 players. Football teams in the Big 10 have 120 players. So this was a potentially massive project. Plus, I only had a three-year leave of absence from the BYU-Hawaii campus and I was kind of looking forward to getting back to the nice weather. He asked me what it would take to get me to help the team. We ended up having a three-hour lunch talking about the psychological aspects of football. He asked me to visit with the athletic director to see if he'd hire me as a full-time sport psychologist. Then I would be able to work with all of the University of Illinois sports departments.

I went in and visited with the director. He had absolutely no interest and said, "I don't want to insult you, Dan, but I think sport psychology is a bunch of bunk. No university has a full-time sport psychologist and we're not going to be the first." I was talking to Mike on my way back out to my car. He said, "Can you wait until Monday before you sign your contract to go back to Hawaii?" I said, "Sure, but what's going to change between now and Monday?" He said, "Well, this weekend is a retreat in Florida for all the Big 10 head football coaches and athletic directors. I'm going to be with Neal (the athletic director) all weekend. I'll work on him."

Sure enough, when I got to my office first thing Monday morning, there was a note saying "Call Neal." So I met with the athletic director again. He said, "I didn't change my mind. I still don't think a whole lot about sport psychology, but I have no choice. I'm offering you a full-time position as sport psychologist." I said, "What do you mean, you have no choice?"

He said, "Mike was offered three NFL head coaching jobs this year, and we told him if he'd stay at Illinois, we'd give him whatever he needed to be successful. He told me over the weekend that he expects me to hire you as a sport psychologist." So, magically, the sport psychology position was created, in one day. It's amazing what a head football coach in a major Big 10 school can do in one day.

It's been very interesting. There are 18 sports at the University of Illinois and I have worked with every one of those sports. I had a lot of good doctoral students, because we also had the top doctoral program in the country in sport psychology. So I developed an internship program.

There were three or four sports that I didn't work directly with because I had outstanding doctoral students with a background in those areas. We really went full out for three years in an extensive psychological training program with every sport we had — with the real emphasis put on football and basketball, for obvious reasons.

As a matter of fact, I've never spent so much time with a team as I did with that football team during those three years.

I was meeting with probably 20 to 30 players individually per week. One on one. Plus I met with all the positions the night before every game. I'd have the offensive line, then the defensive line, then the running backs and so forth, the night before every game to do a pre-game mental preparation exercise with them. I'd talk with the coach ahead of time and he suggested certain things he wanted to emphasize. I'd talk to the defensive line coach, before I met with the players, about certain areas he wanted to emphasize. It was the same with the offensive line coach.

But Did It Work?

It's amazing. In research we say you can't infer cause and effect from correlating data. But we do this in sports all the time. That first year with the Illinois football team, we were seeded sixth in the Big 10, which is exactly where we had finished the year before. But we had some critical

> "The results were startling — we went 9-0 in the Big 10."

young players; and if they played really well, we could be better. It just happened that these critical young players were the people who also received committed psychological training. During spring football, I started doing extensive psychological training with these young men and we had a great year.

How great? We went 9-0 in the Big 10, which means we beat every other team in the conference that year. If you can do that, it's tremendous financial incentive, because you get the granddaddy of all bowl games — the Rose Bowl, the highest-paying bowl game. Even in those days, the payout was $6.2 million. We hadn't been to the Rose Bowl in over twenty years up to that point. You can spend up to $1 million in expenses. We spent all $1 million in expenses that year. We traveled everybody. Every football player on the team, every walk-on, anybody who we could get to go. We went three weeks early and stayed in Newport Beach.

We had a goal that year. Our goal was the Rose Bowl. We didn't talk about what we were going to do in the Rose Bowl. The whole goal was to get to the Rose Bowl.

Now we had the situation where, if we won the Rose Bowl, we would end the season as national champions. The only team that had a chance to be ahead of us was BYU. They hadn't lost a game that year, but we had played a much tougher schedule than they did, so we knew we would get the national championship if we won the Rose Bowl.

> **"When you've had success in an area, try not to change your routines too much."**

But what a disaster that game was! Two nights before the game, 30,000 alumni arrived. When you haven't been to the Rose Bowl in a long time, everybody comes. I was going around to visit with the players the night before the game, but I couldn't get near them because of all the parents and relatives. You couldn't even walk through the lobby; it was impossible. It was an absolute zoo.

And sure enough, we took one of the worst beatings in the history of the Rose Bowl against a team we never should have lost to. We came in undefeated in the Big 10. UCLA had limped in 5-4, having to beat Washington the last game of the season to do it. They'd limped in, but they played all their games in the Rose Bowl that year — it was their own home field. We lost 45-9 in a game that we should never have lost.

There had been a lot of publicity in the Chicago area about this psychological training program. During the off season I received a call from Tony LaRussa, the manager of the White Sox at that time. He was in the hotel about 100 yards from my office. He said, "Can you come over here? I'd like to talk to you about doing a program with the White Sox like you did with Illinois football and basketball." He was very interested. If I had to pick the most outstanding coach I've ever worked with, it might be Tony LaRussa.

He was an unbelievable coach. He was very concerned and very interested in the sport sciences. In addition to myself as sport psychology consultant, we had an exercise physiology consultant and a biomechanics consultant. For two years I implemented a very extensive psychological training program with the White Sox.

The Role of Psychological Testing

That's where I first got interested in doing psychological testing. I had an opportunity to implement a program with them for two years. The same guy who owns the White Sox owns the Chicago Bulls. Consequently, I also worked with the Bulls for a year, which was a disaster. The owner wanted me to do it, but the coaching staff had no interest whatsoever. That's a worst case scenario. The coaches weren't anywhere as committed as Tony was. So I only worked with the Bulls for one year.

About this time, the head football coach at the University of Illinois got in hot water for NCAA violations. The athletic director was fired for misappropriating funds. So I went back on the basketball coaching staff for a year.

I wanted to get an academic position because now I had a Ph.D., but I also wanted to keep coaching basketball. Coaching at Brockport seemed to be the right opportunity; I could be both the head basketball coach and in a tenure track position. I got tenure and senior faculty rank and I started working with the Sabres. My assistant coach was having to run some practices when I was on the road with the Sabres. Then, six years ago, I got a very nice offer from the Indiana Pacers to start a program with them.

I've worked with every type of team, but many of the psychological aspects of recruiting are the same. How important is it to you that you can know what to look for in an athlete? At the professional level, they've experimented with this for years, but doesn't it also apply at the college level? What I'm doing is taking the background that I've had in professional sports and all the years that I was involved in recruiting and put those together to try and determine the psychological skills of an athlete before we ever draft in professional sports or recruit at the college level.

Determining Psychological Fitness

The first important factor is <u>observation.</u> You want to see the player play. In order to develop that player's psychological skills, you must actually see him in a game situation. Most coaches are looking at how high players can jump or how good a shooter they are. Coaches want to know how well players kick or what speed they have. Those things are important; don't get me wrong.

But I think you also want to look at psychological areas. For example, what are a player's mental preparation skills? How does a player handle competitive anxiety? The way you observe this is to watch the player closely in tight, critical situa-

tions. If he's a basketball player, does it all of a sudden look as though he doesn't want the ball anymore? Is he trying to hide? Or is he trying to get the ball even more? In different sports you look for different things.

If you're recruiting one player, don't watch the other players on the court or on the ice or on the field. Watch that one player in those critical situations. That's the player you're recruiting. Watch him or her very, very closely. See how he or she acts in critical situations. Look at their confidence.

Watch when things aren't going well for them. In almost every sport, there are going to be times during that game when things aren't going well for players. Watch very, very closely. How does that individual react when things aren't going well? Do they have negative facial expressions? Do they yell at their teammates? Do they yell at their coach? Or do they play even harder? That's what you'd certainly like to see. What do they do when things aren't going well for them?

Another important concern is <u>concentration.</u> How can you tell how well this player is at concentrating? If you have a very talented athlete, you're probably going to see some blowouts, especially when you recruit a talented basketball player. One person can dominate a game so much that you're going to see some blowouts. What happens in that blowout? Does the player lose focus? Does he quit playing as hard? Or does he continue playing as hard as if it were not a blowout? Does he stay focused? What happens? This is a good way to evaluate concentration skills.

When there's a blowout, especially if they're winning by a big margin, players with poor concentration all of a sudden are "just going through the motions." If he's going to go through the motions in a game, he's also probably going through the motions in practice. He's not real fired up for practice.

Next, observe <u>achievement motivation.</u> One way to look at this is by asking how committed the individual is to the support areas. What about weight lifting? What about conditioning? What about outside practice? Do they practice off the court? Does the player spend time in the gym? Does he spend time on the rink? Does he spend time in the field in the off season? How committed are players?

> **"Players who were committed to the psychological training were the most successful."**

When I worked with the White Sox and the Bulls, the strength coach, Al Vermeil, worked as strength coach for both teams. We became very good friends. We roomed together a lot on the road. One night we sat down and talked about the players. It was unbelievable. The players who were the most committed to his strength program were also the exact same players who were the most committed to my psychological skills training program. When it was like pulling teeth to get certain players to lift weights, these players were also the ones with no interest in doing anything in the psychological skills area. You can infer things from observing other areas of training. If they don't work hard in weight lifting or conditioning or things like that, they probably aren't going to work hard in a lot of other areas as well. If you can pick some areas to examine, that will give you some idea about how hard they work in other situations.

Leadership is More Than Action

<u>Leadership.</u> It's important to know what kind of leadership skills an individual player has. During the game, watch how an individual player reacts to his or her

teammates. Not only that, but look at how receptive the teammates are to that individual. You can find out a lot about a player by seeing how the other players treat him or her.

Do they look like they respect that player? Do they look like they make a good cohesive unit? Or do they not form a cohesive unit? Is this person one of the reasons they don't have a good cohesive unit? Or is this person the reason they do have a good cohesive unit? Observe these things. These are observations that can be very important to know about any player.

Interpersonal skills. This may be the last criteria listed, but it may be the most important of all. Interpersonal skills are very important in a team sport, perhaps not as critical in individual sports, but very critical in a team sport. If Joe doesn't get along with Pete or Pete doesn't get along with Henry or this group never associates with that group and they all think the coach is a jerk, there's no way that team can go out and play to the best of their ability. So look at the interpersonal themes of the team. How do they interact with their coaches? How do they interact with their teammates? These are things that you can observe.

One of the things I used to do was watch basketball players closely during time-outs. What is she or he doing during time-out? Looking all over the place? Does he even know what the coach is saying? Is he kind of daydreaming? I've seen that. Are they really in there? Are they really focused? Are they really watching what coach is doing? Are they maybe even asking questions? I want to know what happens during the time-out. You can tell a lot about a player from those situations.

The coach that hired me to work with the Pacers also coached the San Antonio Spurs. He called me with a major problem. He had a player who he said "could care less" about the time-outs. This player had set the professional record for the largest amount of fines in one season the previous year. I said, "Well, it sounds like fines are not a motivating factor for this guy. You need to find something

> **"Determine what is most motivating to your player and then use that thing as a motivator."**

else." He said, "You're right. I could fine him every single practice he comes late to, every single practice he misses. It wouldn't make one bit of difference. He'd just pay the fine. Money is not a motivational device for him."

We talked for about 45 minutes trying to figure out what could be a motivation device for this guy. That's a real frustrating thing for a coach. Wouldn't you like to know ahead of time that a player has those traits, so you don't have to deal with guys like that during the season? There are ways you can do it. Be good with your observations, especially looking at mental aspects. Most coaches don't emphasize this enough.

Who else can you talk to who will help you learn something about an individual's psychological makeup? When I started coaching, I used to think that the coach was going to be the key person with helpful information about a player. That was not always the case. The coach is probably the worst person to talk to in this area. The coach has a tendency to oversell his player and the reason he or she does this is because it makes the coach look good. If they have a good player who's going on to play college basketball or volleyball or whatever, then it makes the coach look good.

Talk To the People Who <u>Know</u> the Player

> **"Teachers will know the player better than the school counselor. A coach is even better."**

The most important people to talk to may be a player's teachers. Teachers have usually interacted directly with the student and they'll usually give you the most honest evaluation of that individual. I've found that some teachers are hesitant to tell you anything negative about a student for fear of some kind of repercussion from parents or coaches or the student-athlete. Or maybe they want to make sure that they don't say anything that might jeopardize a scholarship. But I think, as a group, they're usually the best to talk to. I used to think counselors were important sources of information but, especially in large school districts, I have found that counselors often won't even know an individual player.

I've had coaches I talked to that give you a real honest evaluation. But I just don't think they all do, and if you don't know the coach and you haven't had experience with them in the past, I'd be a little bit careful about taking what they say as gospel truth.

Being a researcher, I know that concrete measures are critical. If you want to measure something from a psychological standpoint, there had better be concrete measures. You must make sure that you have validity in what you're doing. Validity has been a major problem in questionnaires that have been done in our field over the years. What validity means is that the questionnaire measures what it's supposed to measure. The American Psychological Association guidelines say that every psychological inventory must have validity data on it before it is ever marketed or used. But that is not always the case, especially in sports.

The reason for this is because validity is a lengthy process. The two inventories used most often in professional sports to help in deciding whom to draft and recruit are an inventory called the AMI (developed in the late 1960's) and a psychology inventory called the 16PF, which measures 16 personality factors.

When I first started working with the Sabres, the general manager said to me, "We're going to test, because almost every team in the NHL tests their potential draft choices. What test should we use?" I didn't know what to tell him. There was no valid test for our purposes. We could have used the AMI, but it had been proven not to be valid by the Calgary Flames. Their sport psychologist was a guy named Hap Davis, a friend of mine. And as for the 16PF, the guy who invented it would roll over in his grave if he ever found that coaches were using this to try and predict who they should or should not recruit. That's not even what it was designed for; it was designed for an abnormal population. It isn't even designed for sports. And yet teams were using it.

So I told the coach that there was no good test out there. He suggested that I design one. I had a real strong psychometric background, so I agreed to design a test. But I still don't know whether it's valid. I can predict that it will be a lot more valid than the AMI or 16PF, but I don't know that for sure. I'm going to make no claims until we use it a few years, and then I'll compile validity data on it.

A psychological test has to be theory-based. I have to be able to measure things that are important. For example, if intelligence is not a critical factor in whether that athlete is going to be successful, why have an intelligence scale? When I first started working with professional teams, back 15 years ago when I first started working with the White Sox, I always talked with the coaches, the management, and the veteran players. I wanted to know what they thought were the most mentally related statistics for being successful in professional baseball.

I came up with six areas to test. Now I had to figure out a way to test those six areas. After about 10 years of consulting with professional teams, I came up with six areas. For the first two areas, I already knew of validated tests to test them. One is the ability to handle stress on the ice or on the court. The next area is the self-confidence level, and I also knew of good inventories that were already validated for that. But for the other four areas, I didn't know of any valid instruments, so I had to design an instrument.

I also told the coaches not to take this inventory as gospel just yet. Don't rule out a prospect just because he scores poorly, or don't raise the guy up two levels in the process because he scores high. At the end of the season, we did a final validity test. We were able to prove that this inventory is valid. So we had to be able to <u>measure</u> psychological skills. The questionnaire had to be short. I'd given long questionnaires and the athletes would lose interest. It takes about 15 minutes to take this questionnaire.

> **"Some of the information you collect will be used only as background material."**

One time I had to give the 16PF to the Pacers because the guy who was the part owner was also a psychologist and he wanted the data on it.

It took some of the guys 12 hours to fill out that questionnaire. It measures things that can't possibly be used in recruiting. We know introversion and extroversion are irrelevant to sports participation. A person can be introverted or extroverted and still be a great athlete. Those measures are a waste of time; it measures things that aren't even important.

Test the Honesty of the Test-Taker

> **"Be sure your test instrument includes a validity scale to check consistency in answers."**

The questionnaire should have a lie scale. If you're using the test to predict who you're going to recruit or who you're going to draft, you want to know if they're lying or not. If they're lying, that's important to know because research shows that when an inventory is being used to determine who gets the job and who doesn't, when there's something on the line, you have about 20% social desirability, which means they're lying. So you have to have a lie scale in the inventory because you have to be able to know who's lying.

I've been fortunate. This inventory has only had about a 5% high end lie scale. I'll give you an example of how you construct a lie scale. For instance, you might have a question on a hockey questionnaire that says "I never make a mistake on the ice." Or "I have never made a mistake on the ice." If they answer true to that, then they're probably lying on the rest of the test, too.

So you put a few of those questions in, just enough so that you know whether they're lying or whether they're not. Then if we have one high on the lie scale, I write it right across the bottom (Note: high on the lie scale). Then when we go to the draft, we just don't use that questionnaire as a basis for judging the candidate. It doesn't necessarily mean that the prospect is lying; it just means there's a propensity to lie.

Compare Apples to Apples

When I first started doing interviews with professional athletes — and this is certainly done in college recruiting as well — I found big problems. The interviews were not standardized. A prospect would come in and meet with a very vocal scout who would ask him excellent questions; everybody would feel real good about the interview. The next player would come in and meet with a scout who was not very vocal. The prospect doesn't get asked the same questions; he doesn't even get asked in the same way. In this process, we're trying to compare apples to oranges. You can't compare apples to oranges.

Now I'm in my eleventh year of sitting in on those draft interviews. It's unbelievable the way the NHL does it. We'll bring in every player who is going to get drafted almost anywhere, throughout all the rounds. In about a 3-4 day period of time, we'll interview may be 50-100 players that we're thinking about drafting. They are not real long interviews, but we want to find out something about them.

The whole time I'm sitting there, I'm trying to figure out their psychological skills. I've also got a questionnaire on each prospect, which helps, because we test all of our potential draft choices as well. Have a plan, and have a set of questions ready to use in the interview. Make sure you're not trying to compare apples to oranges. If you ask a player something, you should ask the next player a similar type of question. Ask him in the same way, with the same tone of voice, with the same body language, or else you're not going to be doing a very good comparison.

Observe. Look for a player's involuntary (or "meta") messages in the interview process. Is the person constantly hiding their face? Are they constantly fidgeting or nervous? Look for things that you could pick up in their meta messages. Look at body language and tone of voice. Sometimes you can tell a lot about a person's psychological skills through this.

Concrete evaluations are necessary so player X can be compared with player Y. If you don't have concrete evaluations, like a questionnaire or a structured interview, you can't compare player X to player Y. It's impossible. Have concrete evaluations.

Multiple evaluations are best, because we all have biases. I might say, "Boy, I really like this guy; he really seemed like a player that we'd want to recruit." But my assistant coach, who goes in and sees the same kid, might say, "This kid's terrible. I didn't like this kid's psychological skills at all. I thought he was rude."

I'll give you a pro example. Nine years ago, the draft was in Buffalo. All these 18-year-olds came in to interview with us. Most players are dressed to the hilt, wearing beautiful silk ties and really nice suits. We interviewed one player who was from a farm in southern Alberta. The player came in wearing Levis and a white T-shirt. That's what he wore to the interview. You could tell right off the bat that the general manager was a little bit upset, and that kind of showed in the interview.

But I really liked the kid. He was so genuine in his answers. He wasn't trying to hide anything. He was a real in-touch farm kid. He probably never owned a suit. He had probably never worn a tie in his life.

After the prospect left, the general manager said, "I wouldn't draft him in a million years. How dare he come here without a coat and tie on!" I said, "Wait just a minute. I liked his answers. I thought he was a very genuine person." I went on to say exactly which answers he gave that indicated he would be a good choice and how he had been very honest and sincere, and how I thought he would be excellent for our program. But I never know what they're going to do, come draft time. I left the morning of the draft.

> **"Don't judge a prospect by his looks alone."**

When I got home and checked the draft results, we had taken the farm player in the third round. He's now skating on our number two line. Our number one line is made up of phenomenal veteran players; so he's doing pretty well. He only spent a year back in juniors, which almost everybody does, and only part of a year in the minor league system, which is unbelievable. We got him in the third round. You aren't going to get a third round draft choice that usually becomes that strong, that close. Especially for a guy who wears Levis and a white T-shirt at the interview. It just shows you have to go past the looks of an individual in order to evaluate their mental psyche.

I spent 10 years studying the theories necessary to write the questionnaire and then I actually designed the questionnaire. We started giving it seven years ago to most of our draft choices. The line in the middle of the test indicates the average score for each of the areas that we measure. Remember, those areas are theory-based. I developed them from all kinds of professional sports people, in a variety of different sports.

The Measures of Success

The first thing we measure is the ability to handle sports-related stress. And it has to be <u>sports-related</u> stress. Maybe they're real good at handling sports stress, but not real good at handling academic stress or something else like that. We want to know about their ability to handle sports stress.

We also look at their confidence level. We have a scale that measures how confident they are in relation to their sport. Next, we test their concentration. How good are they at mentally preparing for games? Another area we look at is whether a player is a leader or a follower. We want to know about leadership skills.

> "Make sure you are able to accurately interpret the results of the testing you have conducted."

If you don't know anything about statistics, the printed results may be hard to understand. Each of the little dots is about one standard deviation. So we know that in their ability to handle stress, they were significantly above average. If a player is two standard deviations above the normal in their self-confidence, that's a critical variable. That's a predictor for whether they will be successful in the NHL.

Another measure on the test is "achievement motivation," or how motivated to achieve and excel they are. How much drive do they have to succeed?

I was with our director of player personnel, Don Luce, and I had with me the questionnaires of our top draft choices for the last 4-5 years. These are players in our organization, so we know them very well.

I laid the questionnaires face down on a sheet of paper so he didn't know whose test was whose. I gave him the names of the players. I told him to start with questionnaire number one. It was the Levi's and T-shirt kid. He had the highest score of the group. Then I told him to start at the other end, with the very worst scores. One guy had an extremely low score. He was a first round draft choice, number eight overall. A big, strong defenseman. He could skate unbelievably. Defensemen have to be able to skate backwards well. He could skate unbelievably backwards. He was very strong. But he had no guts. He wouldn't take a hit. He had terrible psychological skills. He's not even in our organization anymore. We paid him an $80,000 signing bonus. He was a first round draft pick. But he didn't last long.

What applications does this questionnaire have for recruiting? This is the future of psychological aspects of recruiting. I don't think it's going to be long before most major universities are going to be using an instrument like this one, or even this instrument, to determine if an individual has the psychological skills to be successful at their level.

I was approached by a Division III coach who said, "I don't have a big budget, but I'd like to test my top 10 guys at least. I don't have budget to test more than that." At about $30 a test, he can test 10 guys for $300. Another coach, the recruiting coordinator for Oklahoma, wanted to test all of their potential recruits in all their sports. He thought $30 a test was a steal for the results he'd get.

If I know a player's psychological skills ahead of time, it's going to mean a great deal as to whether I want that person in my program. If you have an inventory that's valid — remember validity is the key — and you can test these things, then it puts you one step ahead of someone else, because talent is important.

Remember, I said talent was a critical variable. I'm still convinced it is. I had to convince the scouts of that. The scouts with the Sabres, they're a bunch of old school guys that say, "We don't need any psychological training." They

> **"Talent is a critical variable."**

didn't even know what to look at to try and evaluate a player. So I prepared a booklet that all of our scouts get. It tells them how they can determine the psychological skills of a player and who they should interview.

For example, in hockey, a player moves away from home at a young age. Usually goes to live with a landlady, because he's playing junior hockey in Canada. That landlady becomes a critical person to interview. She's been around the player a lot. Coaches need to know exactly how to conduct the interviews and what things they should look at to determine the psychological skills of the player.

I don't know why, but pro hockey is ahead of the other sports in this area in terms of looking at psychological skills in the draft process. But it's going to filter down to other areas, and I think it's really the key to the future in college athletics. If I had to pick two of the six indicators to look at, I'd tell you to examine their confidence level and their achievement motivation, because I know that they are the prime indicators. When I designed this inventory, I didn't know it was going to predict in every area. I thought that maybe one of these scales would be significant as an indicator of psychological strength.

When we administer the tests, we mail the questionnaire to prospects. We have a form letter that goes to every recruit along with the questionnaire. There are instructions included and we ask them to please send it back in the self-addressed envelope. The return rate that we get is unbelievable. Our return rate is almost 100%. It's obvious why we do, because that player knows that he wants to get drafted as high as possible, so of course he's going to send the questionnaire back.

Can You Teach Psychological Strength?

> **"You can improve an athlete's psychological skills."**

The big question is, "What if we find a player who is very talented but he is lacking in these areas?" Remember the example of the absolute lowest guy we had tested. He was a first round draft choice; number eight overall. I spent hundreds of hours with this player, just to get him up to the middle line. His psychological skills have been developed a great deal because of all the extensive counseling I've done with him. He still is never going to have the numbers that another guy has. So it is possible to develop psychological skills. But it's like trying to take a football player who runs a 5 flat in the 40-yard dash and make him into a running back at a Division I school. If he can only run a 5 flat, you're going to have a difficult time with him being a competitive running back. So maybe that's the best analogy to use. Maybe his leg strength in soccer is only a certain level. He can only kick the ball so hard. You could work that strength, that leg, like crazy and just get him up to normal leg strength. But he's never going to be the great kicker that you would like him to be. You can improve psychological skills, but it's difficult to do. If I were a coach, I'd rather draft the guys with high psychological skills. I work with some guys with tremendous psychological skills, and it's real easy and a real pleasure to work with those type of guys.

The year I worked with the Chicago Bulls, Michael Jordan was in his second year. If you remember his saga, that was the year he broke his foot.

In those days, Michael was the whole offense. I remember sitting with him. I did an introductory meeting with every player in the pre-season in Beloit, WI. Our session was on goals. I had to try and help each player to set appropriate goals. I know what goals should be — optimistic and realistic, performance, not outcome-oriented, and changeable. He said to me, "We're talking about scoring. In order for us to win, I have to average over 50 points a game in the playoffs. Last year I averaged 40 something and we lost in the first round."

Here's a young, second-year player telling me that his goal is to break the NBA scoring record and average over 50 points a game that year. But then I'm thinking in my mind, "If anybody can do it, probably Michael can," so I didn't try and tone it down. If anybody remembers the playoffs that year, they opened against Boston. He scored 73 the first game, 60 something the second game, and he did break the NBA record. He <u>did</u> average over 50 points a game. The team still lost in the first round, but he reached his goal.

One of the highest scores I've ever had on my inventory is a young man named Pat LaFontaine. If you know anything about hockey, you know that this player is one of the most psychologically skilled guys in professional hockey. Even though he's been injured and had a lot of other problems, he's really carried the team.

Psychological skills have been critical in his ability to carry the team. If you can draft some guys with very strong psychological skills, and you've got just a minority of guys with weaker skills, the players with high psychological skills tend to pull the team up. But the opposite can happen as well.

If you have very talented kids with poor psychological skills, that's a team that never reaches its potential. Even though you have kids with good psychological skills, if the majority have weak psychological skills, those players tend to pull the team down.

A person who scores real low on the inventory for leadership has a hard time getting along with his teammates. A person who is high in this scale usually has an easier time getting along with his teammates. That's what I've found. Not everybody on the team is going to be a leader. You can have talented, skilled players who aren't leaders. They're not going to be your captain.

Use Tests to Determine Coaching Style

We want to know what the psychological skills of our players are. I'll give the test to the players and then I'll sit down with the coach and say, "Well, this player is strong here, and weak here. This is a kid that you can yell and scream at on the ice and he's going to just play his heart out when you do that." Then we'll look at another player

> "Tailor how you coach players based on what you've learned in testing."

and I'll say, "This is a kid that if you yell and scream at him on the ice, he's going to go into a shell and we'll lose him for a while. When you need to correct him, do it off the ice." The other use of the test is to be able to tailor how you coach players from their strengths and weaknesses.

We have done extensive testing of women's teams and compared their scores to the men's scores. To be honest, I thought in some areas we'd see significant differences between males and females. To my surprise, we haven't. The skills that determine the elite female athlete are the same skills that determine elite male athletes. It tends to be very similar, when you get to the elite level.

For example, we tested the US gymnastics team — men's, women's and rhythmic gymnastics. When I tested an elite college women's volleyball team, we found very similar data. The data isn't drastically different between men and women.

Personality is relatively stable. These are "traits" not "states." They're relatively stable. For example, in determining validity, you have to determine reliability by testing players several years in a row to see if there are big changes. We've found there aren't.

We look at the goal orientation of athletes. For example, when I meet with professional athletes early in the season, I like to meet with them during training camp. Goals are one thing I go over with them, and some of them aren't very goal-oriented.

You'd think a professional athlete would be fairly goal-oriented. Some of their goals are totally outcome-based goals, such as, "I want to be an NBA All-Star" or "I want to win the NBA championship." Those are okay goals at the end of the rainbow. But they also need specific performance-oriented goals, such as, "I want to improve my field goal percentage from 42% to 48%" or "I want to improve my free throw percentage from 70% to 75%" or "I want to be better at defense." We want them to set very specific performance-oriented goals that are evaluative.

What Could We Have Done Differently?

Remember, at Illinois, we had set the Rose Bowl as our goal. We hadn't been to the Rose Bowl in 20-plus years. We had "Rose Bowl" written across the weight lifting area. We had a big "Rose Bowl" sign as they walked out of the locker room. All year long, at every practice and every game, we just drummed "Rose Bowl" into them. No one ever said what was going to happen when we got to the Rose Bowl. That was very evident, because we went there and fizzled.

The other team stayed in their own beds and played on their own field. We should have never lost that game. But it was all mental. Bo Schembechler, when he took Michigan to the Rose Bowl, moved his players to another hotel the last two nights before the game. He wouldn't even tell anybody where they were going. The last two nights they were secluded. He didn't allow any visitors. I think if Illinois ever got back to the Rose Bowl, they'd probably do the same thing.

I often wonder, should we have had a goal of winning the Rose Bowl? Our goal was *getting* to the Rose Bowl. That was certainly a high and lofty goal and a lot of people thought it was an outrageously high goal.

Set the Right Kind of Goals

> **"By focusing on performance-oriented goals, your players can succeed."**

The key is performance-oriented thinking. Remember, I don't even like a goal of "getting to the Rose Bowl" or "winning the Rose Bowl." A good goal for an offensive lineman might be to learn to concentrate harder and get off the snap quicker. Another goal for the lineman might be to learn to stay lower, so that he gets leverage on the defensive lineman. I want those types of goals. Those are the keys. If they do those things and everybody meets their performance-oriented goals, eventually the outcome will take care of itself.

The strength coach at Illinois was a big factor in this process, and he deserves a lot of credit for it. His name was Bill Cross; he's a famous strength coach. Bill was real big into this Rose Bowl goal. It's achievable if we really work hard, and of course, he used it to motivate players. He'd ask a player, "Why are you gutting out that last rep? You're gutting out that last rep for the Rose Bowl."

You take two people and put them in a strength program, one person guts out the last rep, the other doesn't. The one person's going to gain more strength than the other one. So he used it as a motivation device in weight lifting. They do so much weight lifting that I think it carried over into everything else that they do. I don't think it should have been a different goal. That was a very high and lofty goal. That team achieved a lot by getting to the Rose Bowl.

In Summary...

Psychological assessments are a useful tool for recruiting and for coaching. You can begin to determine a player's psychological skills by examining five key areas:

- Observation – examine a player in a game situation to see how he or she reacts to pressure.
- Concentration – does the player keep his or her focus even when the game is a blowout?
- Achievement Motivation – how much does this player want to succeed?
- Leadership – is the player respected by his or her teammates?
- Interpersonal Skills – can the player get along with others?

If you have examined these criteria, you will be in a much better position to determine whether the player you are recruiting will be a good match with your team, your players, and your coaching abilities.

Author Profile: Dan Smith

Dan Smith has over 15 years of recruiting experience on both the Division I and Division III levels. Currently associate professor of physical education at SUNY-Brockport and a mental training consultant with the National Hockey League Buffalo Sabres, Dan's other coaching stops include the University of Illinois, Brigham Young University-Hawaii and SUNY-Brockport.

EFFECTIVE RECRUITING ON A MINIMAL BUDGET

by Susan Summons

I wear many different hats at Miami-Dade Community College. On some days, I have no idea who I am. But I do know when I walk in the gym and pick up the basketball.

I'm originally from Roxbury Community College. I'm a former inner-city kid from the playground who had no idea how I was going to complete my education, be recruited, and understand the recruiting process as a player and as a coach. I've had the fortunate experience of having a great deal of success in my recruiting and coaching career. Most of this success has been achieved despite severe limitations in my available budget. My experience is proof that effective recruiting can be done on a minimal budget.

A couple of years ago, my school experienced firsthand the devastating effect a national disaster can have on a program. I had the unfortunate experience of being right in the middle of Hurricane Andrew. We lost our gym and our facilities, and we had no money to immediately rebuild. It was a complete disaster.

The timing couldn't have been worse. At the Community College level, we recruit players with potential, develop them into Division I candidates and then watch them move on. It's a very tedious task.

At the time that Hurricane Andrew hit, I had an extremely strong recruiting class. Eight of my players directly experienced the effects of the hurricane. Six were out of the city of Miami. Their homes suffered a lot of damage. Our school suffered facility, building, and vehicle damage. At one point, in some areas, the National Guard shut down the city. My first thought and first concern was for the players — not for the program and everything that had been developed over the past six years. My job was to get out, get through the National Guard and find the players. I needed to make sure they had shelter and food. I asked my players if they wanted to leave somehow, to give them the option to go to another institution, because I had no gym. No facilities. No money. They stuck it out. The administration and the athletic directing staff did a phenomenally great job in putting together community support. We arranged to practice at a community center for that entire year. But the community center hadn't escaped damage from Hurricane Andrew.

Most of the time, my 14 players and I used one court with water dripping from the ceiling, where the ceiling had caved in and it hadn't been repaired yet. Not only that, but because our facilities were borrowed, we didn't have priority use of the court. We couldn't get in when we wanted to.

When we did get in, we had to recognize that in the event someone else came in to use the community center, we had to get off the floor. We were very flexible. If water dripped or we got bumped, I moved to a different site or I'd go into a conditioning drill. Flexibility was very important.

Flexibility is the Key

As a recruiter, I think that regardless of what level you're at, you have to have the ability to alter your recruiting behavior. You need to be able to alter your recruiting emotions and modify strategies at the drop of a hat. I know about effective recruiting on a minimal budget, because Miami-Dade has a minimal recruiting budget — it's practically non-existent.

> **"Be able to alter your strategies on a moment's notice."**

When I came to Miami-Dade, I made a decision to set some goals for the program. One of my goals was to make Miami-Dade one of the best community colleges in the country. Then I had to answer the question, "How am I going to accomplish that task?" I have no budget.

I immediately turned my attention to fundraising. I made one of the assistant athletic directors a director of fundraising. I never make a move without meeting with him.

We meet regularly to discuss the various fundraising projects that we've developed to generate money to supplement the minimal recruiting budget, so that we can be just as competitive, or more competitive, as our opponent.

People constantly ask me what fundraising programs we use. We've developed a variety of fundraising events to raise money for the program.

We:
- sell bottles.
- wash cars.
- developed a girls basketball league seven years ago.
- developed a team camp five years ago.
- developed an individual camp four years ago.

We now have four fundraising programs in place that allow us to supplement our budget on an annual basis. We're now in a position to offer a student assistance with tuition, books, and housing.

Money isn't everything, however. I'm an educator first and a coach second.

Keys to Recruiting Success

The first key to success is your integrity as a coach and as a recruiter. Second, remember that the program has marketing and selling points — the college, the coach, the competition.

You have to find out what your selling points are. You have to sell the prospect, no matter what your budget. That is your job.

If you've taken the job, then you are accountable for coming up with a strategy to sell that program, not only to the players you are recruiting, but to yourself. If you sell yourself on the program, you can sell it to anybody.

Why A Player Chooses Your Program

A player chooses your program based on many factors – most of which you can't control, but some that you can. What are the selling points of you as a coach? Ask yourself that question. Maximize your selling points. What are the program's selling points? Does it have a high academic rating?

> **"First, determine what you have to offer a prospect."**

What is the graduation rate? What is the placement rate for employment after graduation? Does it have national exposure? Has it been nationally ranked? Does it have a winning tradition? Does the school provide academic support services and what do they consist of? Do they have computers?

What about the college social atmosphere? Sometimes this area is overlooked; but interestingly enough, players sometimes say, "I'm going to the University of Peak Performance because they've got the best concerts in the winter." It's true.

Students compare your facilities, your program, your academics, your coaching style, your support system, and even the college's living quarters when choosing a school.

Some football players pick an institution because of the social atmosphere. Some basketball players pick an institution because of the social atmosphere. It happens.

Using School Resources to Supplement Your Recruiting

You have no money. What resources are available within the school? You can put together a recruiting package from start to finish. Go to the student activities office.

Any student activities office at any institution should have access to some type of recruiting pamphlet if you don't want to develop one yourself. Go to the admissions office. They, too, have an admission recruiting packet, if you don't want to develop one yourself.

Check to see if on your campus there is a recruitment task force. If there is, they will have various types of recruiting information you can use as inserts.

Another thing you can do is develop a newsletter. Six years ago I developed a newsletter at Miami-Dade. I started out with just 10 schools and I now have 200-300 schools that receive my newsletter every year.

A work study student is responsible for doing the mailing. The newsletter helps the NCAA Division I, II, and III schools learn about our program. It is a vehicle to market the players and the program.

Other Resources You Can Use

• Implement a fundraising program. If you don't know where to start, talk with your athletic director. I will sometimes sit in on meetings and ask questions. Why do you do this? What can we do? What do you think about this fundraising idea? Do you think it would be successful? How much money do you think we can generate from this particular project?

• A recruiter survey. Ask players what kinds of things that they enjoy or that they enjoyed about being recruited. What did they think about the entire recruiting process. What kinds of responses to your survey do you receive? You can find out what works and what doesn't and compare the "bang you got for your bucks."

One student may reply, "The University of Peak Performance wrote me every day." If that student-athlete chose your program, you may find that your correspondence program made the difference. Of course, the new NCAA recruiting rules restrict the amount of literature that can be sent to students. But you can still find out which of your recruiting efforts have been most successful by conducting a recruiter survey.

• Academic graduation and placement rates. Is that a resource? Absolutely. Players want to know what your graduation rate is. They ask, "What are the chances of my graduating from the program? I understand it's tough." Don't do a disservice to the student and say, "No, that's not true. We have adequate support services." Instead, tell them the truth. If the institution is academically tough, let them know that. They can deal with it. They'll have to deal with it. They will be forced to be accountable and to deal with it. You can arrange the right kinds of support services.

• Parents. Recruit the parents. I recruit the parents, the uncle, the aunt, and the dog. Parents are resources. Athletes' behavior has changed dramatically over the last decade.

You need just about every resource you can to maintain their success and performance — not only in the sports arena, but in the classroom as well.

The Effect of the Media on Recruiting

> **"Try to overcome the stereotypes perpetuated by TV."**

Television and media has not made it easy for small schools to recruit on a minimal budget. Because every time you turn on TV, it's another stereotype.

One day, I turned on the TV and Happy Days was on. The story just happened to be about Chachi, who was playing in a basketball game. Chachi was being recruited and the recruiter went through Chachi, bypassing the high school coach.

He sat down with Chachi and said, "I've taken a look at your high school transcript and your grades don't appear to be very good." Chachi said, "Well, do you think I've still got a chance for an athletic scholarship?"

The recruiter said, "Of course. We will put you on what is called the 'academic disadvantaged scholarship program.' And we'll even throw in some sneakers."

As Chachi is leaving the Happy Days restaurant, his girlfriend walks in. He introduces his girlfriend to the recruiter and the recruiter says, "Chachi, is that your girlfriend? What's her name? Does she need a scholarship, too?"

Chachi says, "Coach, I don't think I can leave here without my girlfriend. It would be very difficult." So the recruiter said, "Don't worry, Chachi, she can take the entrance exam. We can offer her a scholarship, too."

You Can Never Be Too Prepared

Determine your program needs by reviewing your budget. If one exists. Assess your budget and non-budget recruiting strategies. Develop strategies. Assess your recruiting strategies and determine your program needs and budget. You have a minimal budget, but you still have to have a successful program. What do you do?

> **"Assess your needs and set priorities for what you want."**

The first key to effective recruiting on a minimal budget is to be prepared. The second is, be prepared. Finally, be prepared. I can't emphasize planning enough.

But you also need to be able to expect the <u>unexpected</u>. You must have the ability to alter your recruiting behavior, strategies, and characteristics.

On one home visit, my visit lasted five hours. The entire time we were there, I was thinking how important it is to change and alter your behavior based on what is occurring with this recruit. You need to be sensitive to what is happening with the player and the parents in the household.

Know Your Competitors' Assets

Know what the competition is. If you're a race car driver, you're going to know what your competition is before you go to the race, and before you're on the starting line. Know your competition.

Research the player you're recruiting. Find out how likely your recruiting is to be successful. If your recruit is averaging 40 points and he or she is receiving mail from every institution in the country, that should give you a pretty good picture of what type of strategy you must use.

Sometimes a recruiter misjudges his or her ability to sign the player. They say, "Well, that player is not coming here. We don't have what it takes. We're not nationally recognized. We're not a high profile program. The player wants to go big time and won't even look at us."

I think if you listen to that, it's the biggest mistake of your life. Recruiting is a state of mind. It's like a water faucet.

Players, when they're being recruited, are up and down at any given moment. At any given moment, if you come in with your presentation, you may be the one to catch them when they're receptive to your presentation.

The Five "Be's" of Recruiting

1. *Be organized.* Know when you're going to call a recruit.
2. *Be prompt.* If you say you're going to mail something to the recruit, make sure the recruit gets it. And follow up. Follow up is critical. If you don't, recruits will ask, "Why didn't you call me?" For some reason, athletes today are more sensitive than ever.
3. *Be honest* with your prospects.
4. *Be professional* and show genuine concern for the well-being of the student-athlete.
5. *Be courteous.*

Once, I was on a home visit, sitting in the living room, and the player's parent offered me a glass of iced tea. I said, "No, thank you, I don't want anything to drink right now." I continued on with the presentation.

The parent came back again for the second time and asked, "Would you like some iced tea?" Again I said, "No, thank you, I'm not thirsty at this time."

> **"Don't accidently aggravate a parent during a visit."**

I could sense that if I didn't take a glass of iced tea from the mother the next time, I may not get to third base. So the third time she came around, I took that glass of iced tea and I sat it down on the table. When I got a chance, I sipped from it. She then brought out some crackers. This is a very small thing, but parents can get insulted when you're in their home and you're recruiting. If they offer you something, it's their way of showing hospitality.

I had the pleasure of visiting with the coach from the University of North Carolina. She told me a story about a player on a campus visit who asked for a cup of iced tea and they gave her iced coffee.

She asked the waiter three times for iced tea and the waiter repeatedly came back with iced coffee. So the next campus visit she went on, she asked for a cup of iced tea. They brought her a cup of iced tea. And that's the institution she signed with. It's seems like a small detail, but it was a big detail to the recruit.

Use Your People Skills – They're Free

Research your recruiting resources. Contact people. Network. If you have a minimal budget, then you may not have money to bring a kid on a visit. Network with people. Get videotape. You have to trust the judgment of your friends, colleagues or network or recommendations.

If you're not in a position to bring prospects to your campus for a visit, being able to sell them on your program through your contacts may persuade the prospects to visit you on their own.

If you sell them, they are going to make arrangements to come to your campus.

Students come to Miami-Dade and visit all the time. I sell them over the phone or, in some cases, I sell them in person and I tell them one thing — when you get here, everything will be just as I told you.

Integrity Is Everything

Maintain integrity while recruiting. Don't tailgate each other over the same vehicle. Recruiting has become such an institution in itself that fighting over prospects can damage your reputation as a recruiter. Don't compete with each other over the same recruit. Maybe exchange information.

> **"Work with other recruiters, not against them."**

It's a competitive situation. I don't know what it is when we're out there recruiting, whether on a minimal budget or a maximum budget. Your prospects are a big secret. Everyone gets hush-hush.

There are enough players and athletes out there to go around. There are no limits on our athletes' performances. Anyone can break into the field of 64 or the field of 16 or the Final Four. Anyone.

It's not just tradition to have one good player on a team or just one solid recruit plus nine other players. The new tradition is 10 solid, bonafide student-athletes in

your program. You can no longer build a tradition with just one, regardless of what sport you're in.

Maintain your integrity. What kind of student-athlete are you recruiting? If you're on a minimal budget, start with the student-athletes in your area. Then you have to look at students just outside your area — perhaps in the suburbs.

Then, if you're fortunate enough to have any out-of-state scholarships, take a look at those candidates.

Examine Your Prospect's Character

What kind of characteristics are you recruiting? Target those types. I like to recruit the <u>person</u>. I don't just recruit the student-athlete. I want to recruit people who have character. Not characters. Because I believe that your people make your program.

Do you have the right attitude? How can you sell a BMW if you like a Mercedes? You can't. You're going to be uncomfortable. The recruit must believe that you, as a coach, believe in the program. If prospects can look at you and see that you believe in the program, you've got their vote.

Your own character is also important. Do you have specific positions about major issues? Are you willing to compromise those positions? Are you willing to compromise because of your budget. What sacrifices will you make because of your budget? If you don't have a specific goal for your program, you might find yourself saying, "Well, I can't recruit that player because I don't have enough funds." If you have specific goals, you have to stick to them. You can't compromise those goals.

Know Your Staff's Strengths (and Their Weaknesses)

Your staff. Does your staff represent your program? If you're in a program with a minimal budget, you have to get the best out of what you have. Utilize the skills and resources of your staff members. Sit down with your staff.

> **"See if other professors can meet the needs your staff can't."**

Delegate specific responsibilities to your staff and have them be accountable for assessing if they complete those tasks. It makes them feel good when they know they've done something. And it helps you by conserving your time and energy. I'm at a community college so I'm not in a position where I can hire a full-time coach and pay a competitive salary and benefits. But I'm fortunate to have an English teacher who helps out whenever possible. Utilize all available resources. Examine your goals. Try to work within that framework.

If you know you're working on a specific budget or no budget at all, but you know you have to have a staff to get the job done, then try to structure it so that your staff can accomplish your goals.

That is, get someone who might be an English teacher who can also handle study hall or monitor study hall for you. Find someone who is willing to be involved and then use their skills.

In order to become effective, you must be affected by your program environment. You can sit down in your office and decide, "I'm just going to have a mediocre program." or "I'm just going to have an average program."

You can make that decision. You need to be affected by your environment, by what's happening around you, by your competitors, and by what the other programs are doing. So get involved. Do you want to be great? Do you want to be good. Do you want to be average? Do you just want to be fair? Your team is a direct result of the coach. If you settle for being average, you won't make it to the Final Four. If you make a decision that you just want to be just good, you may get to the field of 64. It's not guaranteed. What <u>is</u> guaranteed is that you have to make a decision to be great and be competitive.

"Ready Made" Talent vs. "Make Your Own" Talent

Are you willing to take a less skilled athlete and teach and develop his skills, or do you want a ready-made star? When you're recruiting on a minimal budget, you have two choices.

> **"I choose to make my own talent because I can make a difference."**

On the one hand, you're in a position where you perhaps can land a student who's just a phenomenal 6'2" athlete, with minimal skills, waiting to be developed. On the other hand, you have a student who is 6'3" with fantastic skills. She's been recruited by 50 or 60 different colleges and we know, statistically, your chances of landing that student may not be as great as your chances of landing the student who has no skills.

I choose the athlete with promise. One of my players was 6'2-1/2" and the reason I recruited her is because it was within my minimal budget. I was willing to work hard to teach her the game, to make her as competitive as other players who are 6'3" who may have been part of someone's comparable budget.

My player was a small-budget success story. She ended up being the nation's leading rebounder in 1992, averaging 19 rebounds a game. She was ranked third in the nation in scoring and was a two-time Kodak All-American. She also graduated from Miami-Dade with a degree in criminal justice.

When I recruited her, she asked me a question I am frequently asked, "What are the chances of getting exposure to a program that may give us the opportunity to go pro?" My response is simply, let's take it step by step. Let's deal with the academics first. Let's deal with the development of your skill level and let the other long-term goals take care of themselves.

How Can You Most Effectively "Market" Your Program?

Are you willing to take a less skilled athlete and teach them the game? Ten players are worth more than one diamond in the 90s. Entrepreneurs never stop looking for ways to enhance and market their business.

Recruiters must also always be looking for ways to enhance and market our programs. Get involved. You must like to recruit and you must like the recruiting concept. There's nothing worse than to be a player being recruited by someone who doesn't like to recruit or who doesn't believe in his or her program.

Football player, basketball player, baseball player — it doesn't matter. That player is going to look at you, and know there's no interest.

What Kinds of Athletes Should You Be Recruiting?

A 10-year trend has seen a change in types of athletes seeking athletic scholarships. As a result, you must adjust to the now and the future. Whatever happened to playing a game for fun? I can remember playing on the field and I just had a lot of fun. It was no big deal. Statistics weren't important. What was important was that the team won and we were having fun doing it.

Attitude Is Everything

> **"Look for players who aren't just thinking of themselves."**

Whatever happened to the appreciation of receiving a scholarship? The player has changed. The game has changed. What was once a joy is now old news.

I talk to recruits and they say, "Well, how many pairs of sneakers am I going to get?" I tell them, "None."

Behavior is learned. Somewhere along the way, someone told that recruit they were going to get two or three pairs of sneakers. Otherwise, why would they say it? Why would they know to say it and feel comfortable saying it? Conditioning. Dedication.

The players ask, "What do I get out of it?" I tell them, "You get an education." They want more. As recruiters, we are in a prime position to control that. We can change their impression. We can change that emotion. We can set them straight. We have a responsibility to set the record straight. This is a whole new type of student-athlete who is emerging in this decade, and we need to be prepared to meet their needs. Television and media don't help. Dr. Robert Singer, a famous sports psychologist, talks about how athletes thrive on extrinsic rewards of competition.

Our athletes today in the recruiting institution, whether you are on a minimal budget or a comparable budget, are thriving off of expensive rewards. Somehow we've got to change that. As a coach, I may never get the player I want. I think it's important to consider the integrity of the program and the professional.

Is there a compromise? If you do compromise, what have you become? You have to ask yourself how important your integrity is to the well-being of the program, the institution, and the administrators you represent. Can you look at yourself in the mirror?

Know Your Limits

What are you willing to do? How far are you willing to go before you sell yourself out as a person, as a coach? Before you sell your integrity? An effective coach believes in himself, his program and his recruiting abilities.

Stay away from gossip. Deal with facts. For instance, you may hear a rumor that you will not be able to recruit four athletes because you heard that they are signing with another university. When we do that, we fall into the gossip trap and don't recruit.

I experienced this situation. I went after the four recruits and interestingly enough, we signed all four. I don't know if I was just lucky or if I did a heck of a job selling them, or it was just my day, or the water faucet was running, or they just had a minute where I got in.

They happened to be from a program that was ranked in the top 25 of the USA Today poll for high school basketball, and three of them happened to be post players, which is the position that I was looking for. And it was in the county area. I recruited them all with a minimal budget. That's the lesson. Stay away from gossip. Deal with facts.

Recruit To Your Ideal Standard

Most importantly, recruit the player you need and want, and maintain contact to develop a successful recruiting situation. If you're recruiting on a minimal budget and you establish a recruiting situation with the high school, with the community person, the youth director, or whomever you're dealing with, maintain it.

> "Keep in contact with a prospect to keep your program in consideration."

The worst thing you can do is recruit well and the following year don't send them anything. You don't call them; you don't do anything. They may be offended. They may feel you're not interested. If nothing else, send them a letter, asking, "How are you? I wanted to drop you a note to see how you are doing. How's the team this year?" They respond, "We're great, but we really don't have any top recruits." Be confident. Be prepared.

Get Involved To Get Recruits

Community involvement is important. One of the selling points of our program is that I'm involved in the community. I'm a regional director for the National Shoot for the Stars program for Miami youth.

One of the best ways to be visible to prospective recruits is to get involved. I travel around to different organizations, youth groups, and I speak.

We also do development training, and I bring my students. I make it a requirement that my players put in community service hours. Parents love to hear that their kids are getting involved in the community. It's a great selling tool. In exchange for our involvement, we get involved with the corporate education program and the players are able to attend the Miami Heat games on complimentary passes.

One key factor is your program, especially the campus visit and the home visit. When the recruit comes to your campus, try to maximize the visit, within reason and within your parameters, of course. Recruit student-athletes with character. Don't compromise your standards. Recruit from a winning program, because you tend to share similar characteristics.

The Pyramid of Success

John Wooden developed a pyramid of success. He spent all of his energy being concerned about the performance, the development, training, and recruiting his team. He wasn't concerned by his opponents. Period. The message is, "Be more concerned about your own program than what others are doing."

If you want to be effective recruiting on a minimal budget, do not worry about your opponents. Be more focused on maximizing your high points, developing your selling points and enhancing your program. Do the best that you can. Maintain your integrity and you will still have the edge in effective recruiting on a minimal budget.

Author Profile: Susan Summons

Susan Summons is the head women's basketball coach and associate professor of physical education at Miami-Dade Community College Kendall Campus. She has 17 years of experience as head coach, teacher, administrator and academic advisor at the community college level. A national coach-of-the-year winner in both Florida and Massachusetts, she has also been on the staff of USA Basketball, the Goodwill Games, World Scholar-Athlete Games and the U.S. Olympic Festival.

RECRUITING FROM THE BOTTOM UP: STARTING A PROGRAM FROM SCRATCH

by Bob Warming

If you continue to coach, at one time or another, you're going to coach some-place other than where you are now. When that happens, you're going to feel like you're starting from scratch.

I've been at seven different institutions during the last 21 years. "Recruiting from the Bottom Up" is all about developing a recruiting process for your program when you're starting from scratch.

I learned these techniques the hard way — from experience — when I reacti-vated the soccer program at Creighton University. Before I began at Creighton, I was at the University of North Carolina–Charlotte for seven years as head coach. We won the conference championship in 1988 and 1989.

After that, Doug Elgin, a commissioner of the Missouri Valley Conference, called me and said, "Bob, Creighton University is one of the programs in the Missouri Valley Conference and they are starting a program from scratch. I'd like to recom-mend you for the job." He went on to tell me about the school and the athletic director and what a great place Omaha was, especially what a wonderful place it was to raise a family. I said, "Doug, that's great, but I've never really wanted to live in Oklahoma." I had no idea that Omaha was in Nebraska. He said, "Bob, you won't have to live in Oklahoma; you can live in Nebraska, because that's where Creighton is."

So I got out the map and figured out exactly where Omaha was and told my wife that Doug had recommended me for a job and it sounded like an interesting opportunity and I'd like to go out and visit with the people about it. I said that I would fly out for a one-day interview and fly back the same day.

I called my wife from the airport the night of the interview process and she said, "Well, are you about ready to come home?"
I said, "Honey, I decided not to get on the plane. I want to stick around for a little while and take a look at the place and see what Omaha is about."

I told her I had a great talk with the athletic director and the president of the university, as well as other people at the university, and I wanted to check out Omaha a little bit.

The next night, I called her and she asked, "Where are you?" "I'm in Omaha," I replied. There was dead silence on the other end of the line. She said, "Why aren't you home?" I told her I really liked the town, the university, and what they were doing, and that I wanted to look at some houses the next day. When I told her I thought they might offer me the job and if they did, that I was going to consider it, she hung up on me.

The bottom line is they did offer me the job the next day. I flew my wife out and she fell in love with the place, too. I share that story because I was being recruited by an institution that I knew little about; I didn't even know its location. Then I met the people in Omaha and they made such a terrific impression on me, that I went from being very happy where I was to deciding to pick up and move to a place out in the middle of the United States.

That's what your challenge is as a recruiter: to figure out what it is that will make players want to come to your school or university, even though they may not know anything about you. The answer is the *people,* as far as I'm concerned. It's all about the people the recruit talks to.

It's also about the impression that the university makes on prospects through campus visits and personal contacts.

What's Your Vision?

> "Know what you want, and what the school and community wants."

The first thing is to develop a vision of what it is you really want to do with a job. I think there are three important sources of input for that. One is what the university wants. Two is what you, as a coach, want. Three is what the community wants. Those things don't always match up.

I took the job at Creighton. The gentleman who hired me, the vice president, left before we ever got started. The budget and everything else within the university changed. I knew what I wanted to do with the program. It was pretty clear that the university's perspective had changed a little bit from when I'd been hired.

I'd been out in the community during the first six months of the job, getting people excited about what we were going to do, but their expectations were a great deal higher maybe than the commitment the university was going to make.

Having a Vision and a Mission

My vision led to a mission for the program. I knew what I wanted to do, which was to make a team that would be competitive for a national championship. Having convinced people in the community that this was something we were going to try to do helped us to raise the money to go out and recruit what I felt at the time were some of the better players in the country.

The University wanted certain specific things out of the program. They had dropped the soccer program five years before I took over. They completely cut it out. They'd had players who had stolen a university van and driven it right into the river during a drunken party one night. They'd torn up dormitories. They'd torn up motel rooms. They had some real problems and decided to drop the program.

So I knew one of the things the university wanted and had to have for our program to grow and be successful — for them to continue to give any kind of commitment to the program — was good people involved in the program. They wanted the right kind of guys involved in the program. That was a real challenge to me.

I went out and I saw some players who were pretty good players, but they didn't have the character that I wanted for the program. I really felt that character was going to be the key issue in order for the university to continue to make a commitment to our program. I had to find people of the right character.

Make Connections in the Community

I did that from the moment I started recruiting people. I told them we were going to make a commitment to the university. By that, I meant the players on the team — they were going to make a commitment to their academic success and they were going to make a commitment to others outside the university, outside their academic success. They were going to make a commitment to other people in our community.

> **"Start by having your athletes make a commitment to the program."**

How did we reach out to the community? We talked to children in elementary schools. We spoke to over 7,000 children in elementary schools around the city of Omaha. We ran free clinics and camps for children during the year. We talked to them about healthy lifestyles and setting goals. In short, we were trying to accomplish the things that we felt were very important for the youth of America.

Our players were great role models. They had achieved a lot. They had obtained a scholarship to Creighton University. They had achieved well enough academically to go to a very difficult school, like Creighton. We wanted the players to go out and spread that message. This has become one of the key factors as to why players end up coming to our school.

Every time a player visits during a recruiting trip, we make sure it is during a time when our kids are out speaking in the community or participating in some community event. Or we plan a visit in conjunction with a home game, because our players spend at least 30 to 45 minutes after every game signing autographs for the kids in the community.

Community service has become the greatest recruiting tool for us. It is the mission of Creighton University. Service to others has become something that I'm very proud of because our former players who have graduated are now continuing to do it in the communities where they live.

The Impact of Community Connections

> **"Get your athletes involved in the community."**

I had an article on the door of my office that was faxed to me by one of the players I recruited in the very first class. His name was Brian and he was a three-time All-American at Creighton during his sophomore, junior, and senior years. He is now playing in Richmond in the USISL league. The article was about how Brian had visited an elementary school every single day that school was in session during the month of May. He talked with the children about healthy lifestyles and goal setting, and the things that were important to him. He hoped to make it important to them. There's something special about Brian and his fellow players who graduated from that class of 1993.

That 1993 team was number one in the country. We were the first undefeated team in 20 years at the school, before we ran into the Air Force Academy team in the playoffs. All the kids on that team are continuing to do positive things for their communities today.

Selecting Team Players

We have developed a vision of what will make our institution special in the minds of parents and in players. The question becomes, "How can you recruit players with no history to show?"

At Creighton, obviously, we didn't have a team when I started. I would take some players out to where we were going to play. We'd stand in the middle of the field and we'd talk about what was going to happen. We talked about how we were going to fill the stadium and where they were going to score the goals from, and what was going to happen. I went through the whole thing with them. Some days it was a little cold and windy and they lost faith.

There were times when some of the guys would succumb to doubt and say, "Yeah, right, Coach. Let's go get something to eat. That's a nice story."

Some guys stayed there and dreamed. Every guy who listened and dreamed, we signed in that first class. Every single player who visualized it, who imagined it, who was sold in his mind on that story about what we were going to do with the program, came and were very successful. They made us the number one team in the country.

I think you have to do the same kind of thing when you go into a new program. Give them that same kind of vision. You can only show them what you've done at other schools. You can't show them what you've done at that school, because it hasn't happened yet. You have to have them imagine that it is possible and visualize it becoming reality.

Truth is Sometimes Stranger Than Fiction

I have to tell you at least a few recruiting stories because there's no truth without a story behind it. I did a lot of recruiting in Texas . This story happened as our budget began to run out toward the end of the year.

I did a lot of driving from Omaha down to Texas. In fact, I drove down almost every weekend. In one particular instance, I was recruiting a boy named Ray from Grapevine, Texas, who became our all-time assist leader.

I was talking to the coach at Grapevine and he said, "Bob, we have a team down at South Texas, a high school team, that's been undefeated for the last three years. They're way down on the border next to Mexico, but you probably ought to go down there and see them."

I started off driving early in the morning. I drove all the way down to Southwest Texas. Way off over in the distance I saw some lights. It was an old wooden stadium, open on both ends behind the goals. There were old, wooden 10-row bleachers lining both sides of the stadium and they were jam-packed. People were cheering and chanting; everybody was just going crazy, getting ready for the game to start.

I got in, found a place to squeeze into a seat, sat down, and started getting myself comfortable.

I looked down and at each end, behind the goals, there were about a dozen state troopers lined up behind each goal. I asked the guy next to me, "What are those state troopers doing down there?" He replied, "We shoot anybody that tries to get in." That was all right. I had paid for my ticket. I was pretty comfortable.

About 10 minutes into the game, I was beginning to think that the home team was really not very good. Certainly the team from Houston was playing a heck of a lot better.

All of a sudden behind one goal, I heard a noise: "bam-bam-bam." Everybody

in the crowd started cheering. They were going crazy. There were about six state troopers with their guns pointed and they were shooting! The place started going bananas. The home team manager picked up a garden rake and went sprinting down to the end of the field. He went behind the goal and scooped up a big rattlesnake. He held it up in the air and the crowd went crazy again. Everybody stood up and started cheering.

The guy sitting next to me said, "We're going to win tonight." I'm thinking it's some kind of superstition or something, but I guess the lights are drawing these big rattlesnakes from out in the desert area. About 10 minutes later, they do it again — "bam bam bam," — this time, down at the other end of the field, the state troopers are all shooting at rattlesnakes. The crowd went nuts again.

Sure enough, the manager picked up a big garden rake, ran down to the other end of the field, and scooped up a snake about six feet long. And the place went bananas again. Everybody started chanting and cheering about the rattlesnake. It was an unbelievable experience.

Right before half time, the visiting team scored a goal and went ahead one to zero. Both teams retreated to the locker room. About five minutes later, the lights on some of the state troopers cars light up and they take off.

At the start of the second half, there were a dozen state troopers behind the home team goalkeeper. At the other end of the field, there was not a soul. Nobody was down there.

The home team won six to one. I don't think the away-team goalie ever saw a single ball go in the net. That's a true story.

So sometimes you go someplace thinking you're going to recruit somebody with an outstanding record and you think it's because they must have a lot of great players. Then you get there and you find out there are some other factors involved in the program that are accounting for the team's success.

Selecting the Cream of the Crop

> "You can't find out what you need to know about a prospect on paper."

You have to really focus on the kind of people that fit into your program. I get about 25 of pieces of mail every-day from outfits like the National Recruiting Service with a picture of a guy on it and all his statistics. We respond to everybody at Creighton; we have a form letter we send those guys.

Player sheets are the biggest ripoff and I'll tell you why. It's because I believe that you want your program to be like a "river" — a river with banks, or bound-aries, designating what you want your program to be like. A river without banks is just a puddle. No one wants to be hanging around puddles. You get mosquitoes and all kinds of other stuff.

You want a program to be very narrow in its focus about where you're trying to lead it. I think things like player sheets are all huge distractions. They're time-con-suming and they're distracting.

If you want to know where the good players are, and who they are, you need to go out and see them. But a piece of paper with a kid's picture and statistics on it is all part of stuff that you don't want to be involved with.

You want to have a very narrow focus on exactly who you want in your program. Determine exactly the kind of people you want to have playing for you. Go see the players and get to know them on a personal level. Get to know everything about them that you can.

Get Rid of Your Preconceived Ideas

Once you start identifying the kind of people you want in your program, you need to set up everything involved to get to know them, and so that they can get to know you, and what your program is all about.

You want to have everything you're doing to include positive words, a positive environment, and positive people. This is especially true when they finally come to your campus for a visit. Before I'd been to Nebraska, my only vision of the state was based on a guy I'd met who was from there, and he'd had blonde hair and "blue ears." I knew it was cold there. I knew there were some problems there.

That's what I was expecting when I came to Nebraska. When I came out here in June, I didn't know if I would need an overcoat. The guy who brought me to the campus took me into the entrance to the university and the flowers were in bloom and the grass had been freshly cut and everything looked great. The very first people that I met were very high energy, positive people who wanted success for the soccer program.

That's why I think the *people* aspect of recruiting is so important. You've heard, "You never get a second chance to make a first impression." No where is that expression more true than in the college recruiting process. People make assumptions and you can't change their mind no matter how much you try.

Develop a System

When you're recruiting from the bottom up, you don't have to deal with any preconceived notions about what a recruiting visit to your campus should or should not be. Instead, you can develop your own system.

> "You can develop a system that works for you and that meets your needs."

I've taken every recruit that we've had on campus on exactly the same path as when I was brought in. They take exactly the same route from the airport, they come in at exactly the same spot and they meet some of the same people that I did when I first came to campus. I liked my "recruiting" experience when they were trying to get me to the campus so much that I try and replicate it for our recruits, too. One of the guys that they always met right at the first was our team physician, Dr. Lee Bevilacqua. We called him "Doc B". Every time a kid met him, the very first thing he did as he shook their hand, was that he said, "How do you like me so far?" It brought a smile to their face and they already had in mind that he must be a pretty good guy.

The very first thing that happens with players when you bring them on your campus has to be incredibly positive.

If you have some telephone calls to make to prospective recruits, you had better not get on the phone unless you're hyped up.

Whatever it is you have to do to make yourself "ready to go" when you get on the phone, you better do it.

When they see you on the phone to another recruit, that's their image of you, how you are on the phone at that one time during the week.

Repeat Contact With Prospects is an Essential Part of the Process

> **"Without results, all you have is your vision. But that may be all you need."**

When you are starting a program from the bottom up, prospects don't have any idea of how you will develop the program. If you have worked in other programs, they may be able to get an idea of how your system works, based on your past performance, but they can't be sure.

As you know, part of any program's system is completely separate from the coach and its recruiters. Prospects don't know if what they saw when you were coaching at another school was *your* style particularly, or a function of the system that was developed long before you got there.

So when you start from scratch, you need to convince prospects of your vision, and that process takes time.

Know the Rules – Both the Written and Unwritten Ones

In any program, there are a series of rules that the coach and the coaching staff must follow. Obviously, there are NCAA, NAIA and other divisional rules, but there are also school-imposed rules as well. First, you have to consider the basic divisional rules when developing your program.

I could never have built the team we built at Creighton University under the current rules. For example, when I was recruiting one of our players, Brian, who ended up a three-time All American, he told me from the very first phone call, "Coach, I'm not coming to Creighton."

I called him every night for six straight months. Every single night. I had accepted that he wasn't sold on the program the very first time I talked to him. I said, "Brian, that's okay. I really like you though and I just want to talk with you." He agreed to let me keep in touch with him just to see what was going on in his life. He'd already taken four official visits, to UCLA, Virginia, North Carolina and George Mason. Several schools from the ACC wanted him. I said "Brian, it's supposed to be real nice up here next weekend. Why don't you and your dad drive up on an unofficial visit?" He asked, "Will you quit calling me if I do that?" I said, "Do you want me to quit calling you?" He said, "Yes!" but he agreed to come and see me.

He came up on the unofficial visit. We had a great visit and when they left, he and his dad said, "We would like to come again next week on an official visit."

He took his official visit the following week, which was three weeks before the signing date, and we were able to sign him right after that. He was very happy at Creighton, and I was happy that I hadn't given up on him too soon.

You can't take no for an answer and you have to be upbeat and positive with them the whole time. Eventually it will pay off for you.

When we signed Brian there was no question he was going to get us on the river and get us going quickly downstream. He led us right to the mouth of where we wanted to have our program be. I was going to make sure we got that player in our program, because I knew he'd like our program and what it had to offer him, if only I could get the opportunity to show him that in person.

Becoming a "Known" Quantity in the Eyes of Your Prospects

Brian's experience was very similar to mine, of not really knowing much about Creighton University. When you develop a program from scratch, you are an unknown quantity — prospects don't know what you have to offer, and even the people who are advising them — parents, coaches, and friends — can't give them any answers or

> "The greatest challenge is becoming a 'known' quantity."

guarantees that they will like the program. Of course, no one can guarantee that any player will be happy with their decision, even if the program has been around for decades.

But another disadvantage of building a program from scratch is when the university that you are coaching for is also an unknown quantity. Creighton had been inactive for a period of several years. They hadn't been particularly well-known even when they did have a program.

Both of these factors worked against us in recruiting, because people like to see a track record when they buy anything, and that's particularly true when you're not just committing playing time for a sport, but your entire college education! Whatever you can do to bring the prospect in and get him or her involved, do it.

For example, Brian was a huge Walt Disney fan. When he came up to visit Creighton, we went to see a Disney movie. He enjoyed it. He had a great time. Every place that was recruiting him was telling him the same thing I was telling him: "We're going to win the national championship and you're going to help us do it." There was no question about that.

With the kind of player Brian was, he would be a great asset to any team – and I knew he'd make a world of difference on our team.

However, we were competing against some great schools that wanted to sign him. They had better facilities than we did. We're never going to wow people with our facilities. We knew that from the beginning. So I tried a different, more personal approach.

When I asked him two years later what really made him choose Creighton, he said he felt like he was going to have a lot of fun there.

When you're dealing with guys 17 years old, you can tell him about how this is a great program and how it's going to be, but if they don't think they're going to have fun, they may not come. Sometimes you need more than just a convincing sales pitch. These players are used to pie-in-the-sky dreams. But they know that the pitch doesn't always meet reality. Players always have someone to remind them of that.

That individual who helps a prospect evaluate the program objectively is a key component for any recruiter, whether you are starting from scratch or not. With Brian and with many of our other players, finding what I call "the champion" is a difficult part of the recruiting process, but it's essential.

Identify Your Player's "Champion"

> "The 'champion' will guide you to where you need to go with a prospect."

The champion is the person who sways the recruit's influence the most. Sometimes it's the mother, sometimes it's the father. That's a pretty quick one to figure out for you. Sometimes it's a sister, a brother, or somebody in the community. Maybe it's the coach. No matter whoever that person is, the champion has to be part of your narrow focus, too. You need to make a personal connection with that individual, just as you do with the player.

Once you figure out who that person is, it's going to keep you on the river, and help guide you where you want to go. Do everything you can with that one person.

Send your form letters out and do whatever else you usually do with the other people who are involved around the player's periphery.

But for the one person who's going to help that young person make a decision, really develop a relationship with that person, because it's going to be awfully difficult for that person, as well as the player, to tell you no.

On another one of those trips to Texas, I was driving through Oklahoma. I have one quirk: I'll talk to anybody. While I was there, I pulled into a gas station. The attendant asked me as he cleaned off my windshield what I was doing and I told him I was from Creighton University and starting a soccer program from scratch.

He said, "Son, we got the best soccer player you've ever seen. He's right across the street, right here in Oklahoma. You just go over there and see that boy. In fact, they're playing over at the high school right across the street right now."

So I decided to see what he was talking about. After all, I had driven all this way anyway. I entered the high school parking lot and went into the stadium. I watched the game for about five minutes and there was no question about who the man had been talking about. There was one player, he had to be 6'4" or 6'5". He's scoring goals at one end of the field, and it is unbelievable. His team is terrible, but he is incredible. He was sprinting back to the other end of the field and he's clearing balls off the line, saving his team from being scored on. Then he's sprinting down the other end of the field and making goals. No one can stop him.

I just couldn't wait for the game to be over because I thought I had found a franchise player. As soon as the game was over, I ran down to the field, went around to the stadium, hopped over the hedge, and talked to the coach. I told him who I was and what I was doing there and I asked him about his players. I told him that there was one guy in particular I'd really like to talk to.

He said to me, "You mean the big boy." I said, "Yeah, I have to see him." The coach told me he was about to get on the bus. I ran across the field, and just before the boy gets on the bus, I grabbed him by the shoulder. I asked him how he was doing, and I introduced myself to him. I told him, "I think you're a terrific player. I think you're unbelievable. And I'd really love to have you as part of our program." I told him I'd just like to talk with him a few minutes, and I asked the driver to hold the bus here for a few minutes. The bus driver agreed and so I took the player aside to talk to him.

> **"Make sure a prospect can meet academic requirements."**

I told the player, "I just want to tell you a little bit more about our program. I'd really like to have you come for a visit and talk with you about our school, and have you help us win a national championship." He said "Okay." I said, 'Son, you're so much bigger than everybody else out there on the field. Are you a little older than everybody else?" After counting on his fingers, he said, "Uhm, I'm 17 sir."

I said, "Well, you're a lot bigger than everybody else. How tall are you? You've got to be 6'4" or 6'5", aren't you?" After placing his hand above his head, he said, "Uhm, yeah, I'm 6'5"."

I'm a pretty bright guy. I'm already starting to figure maybe this guy isn't made for Creighton, because we have very high academic admission requirements, but I said, "Son, what's your name? I want to keep your name on file. I want to continue to visit with you."

After a moment of bobbing his head up and down, he told me his name was Larry. I said, "Great, Larry. I understand this business with counting on your fingers about your age. I understand about using your hand to tell me how tall you are, but what's this thing with your head, when I asked you about your name?" He said, "That's easy sir. That's the way I remember my name — 'Happy birthday to you, happy birthday to you. Happy Birthday, dear Larry, happy birthday to you.'"

I found out later that Larry is a pretty good football player and he went to Oklahoma and played football there on an academic scholarship. The key to me, in this process, is to figure out a way to make your program a fun place to be and a special place to be for the players.

All Work and No Play...

To make it fun for players, I prefer being positive with people. I tried to create an environment that was very positive for our prospects whenever they come to campus. We never let them anywhere or near anybody who is negative.

One of the keys for success with our program was that I made it a point everyday to remind our players how fortunate they were to be at Creighton University.

An "Attitude of Gratitude"

> "There are things to complain about at every school."

Every single one of our players believed they were fortunate to be at Creighton. They were living every single day with an attitude of gratitude.

I don't know if you've been by Creighton's campus, but it's in the middle of downtown Omaha. You only have to go four blocks north of us if you want to see where there are people who are not as fortunate as our kids.

There are always things to complain about in any school. The don't like the food. The dorms aren't something to write home about. There's always something to complain about. But as a leader of the program you have to make sure that every single player has a positive feeling about where they are.

You really have to make sure that your players on the team don't feel negative. They are lucky. They are so fortunate to be where they are. But you have to keep emphasizing that.

Think about it from their perspective. College is supposed to be fun and it's supposed to be a special place to be. I think it's special to be at our school because one, our players believe they're lucky to be there. And two, because of how we've structured our program, they've been out in the community doing something special for children, which in turn made them feel more special about themselves. We felt good about ourselves when we helped other people, and when we believed (or at least perceived) that we were fortunate for being able to help others.

The last thing I'd have to tell you about making your vision of what you, your university and the community wants is that you have to make sure that every single person that you recruit in the program is one you'd take home to your mother. What I mean by that is that every prospect should be what I call "a great kid."

In 20 years of doing this, I have compromised my belief on this point several times. During my last year at UNC-Charlotte, we won our conference. We defeated

Duke and had received about 20 Top Ten votes in the country. However, I had some kids on that team that I was not proud of, and I hated every single second of the year. I found that it wasn't worth compromising my beliefs about the types of players that I wanted to recruit, because then *I* wasn't having fun. If I wasn't having fun, it was pretty difficult to convince the players to have fun. And if I am the one making the choices about the types of players that will be a part of my program, I'm going to stick to my beliefs and choose the players who I could feel comfortable taking home to meet my mom.

Anybody who is coaching is not doing it for the money because there are a lot of ways that any of us could make a lot more money. The hours are long and it requires a lot of energy. Beyond that, it also requires enthusiasm and a genuine belief in yourself, your players and your program. If you are going to give of yourself as a coach, you'd better be receiving rewards in the form of personal satisfaction.

I'm sure I'm not alone in saying that I have been approached by a lot of people who think they can help us coaches make a lot more money than we're making now. What they don't realize is that I'm in it for more than the money. Sure, I want my family to be able to eat and have a place to live. But I also want to leave an impression on my players. I want to help them make something of their lives. That's more important than making a bunch of money.

When you're developing your program from scratch, you have the opportunity to create just the type of program that you will be proud of and that can make an impression on your players. Get people in your program that you'll be proud of. Get people in your program who are committed to the same things you are. Believe me – your program will overachieve every time.

Author Profile: Bob Warming

Bob Warming is head men's soccer coach at Saint Louis University. Bob has 22 years of recruiting experience on the NAIA and NCAA Division I levels. A national, regional or conference coach-of-the-year award winner 10 times in his career, his other coaching stops include Transylvania University, Berry College, University of North Carolina-Charlotte, Creighton University and Old Dominion University. He also held the position of athletic director at Furman University.

THE MENTAL EDGE BOOKSTORE

Competitive Excellence: The Psychology
and Strategy of Successful Team Building (Second Edition)
Retail: $23.95
Your Price: $21.95

A national best seller! A collection of top coaches from across the United States. Each coach is highlighted in sections on motivation, team cohesion, discipline, mental preparation, mental toughness, and communication. A valuable addition to every coach's library!

Basketball Resource Guide
(Second Edition)
Retail: $25.00
Your Price: $22.00

The most comprehensive resource medium for the sport of basketball. Includes listings for audiovisual tapes, books, magazines, research studies and more…The consummate book for the basketball junkie! *NOTE: Third edition is now available on computer disk only. Please inquire for further details.*

The Mental Edge: Basketball's
Peak Performance Workbook (Second Edition)
Retail: $29.95
Your Price: $26.95

The best mental training book for basketball on the market today! A step-by-step manual, teaching mental preparation and training for coaches and athletes. Chapters include goal setting, visualization, stress management, concentration and more…

Psychology of Winning
Notebook
Retail: $25.00
Your Price: $20.00

The complete notes from Steve Brennan's highly-acclaimed Psychology of Winning Clinic. Topics include motivation, discipline and mental toughness. So organized, it's just like being at the clinic!

Golf Psychology
Workbook
Retail: $25.00
Your Price: $22.00

The core text of Steve Brennan's Golf Psychology Workshop for the Competitive Golfer. An in-depth exploration of the mental side of golf for someone who takes the game seriously. It could help you drop a few strokes from your game!

Mental Edge Clinic
Workbook
Retail: $30.00
Your Price: $25.00

The core text of Steve Brennan's nationally-acclaimed Winner's Edge Clinic for coaches and athletes. A tabbed, 3-ring binder containing the most recent research in the field of performance enhancement. Includes an Appendix section, including an extensive list of bibliographical data.

THE MENTAL EDGE BOOKSTORE
Preferred Customer Order Form

BOOKS	QTY.	UNIT PRICE	TOTAL
Competitive Excellence	_____	$21.95	_____
Basketball Resource Guide	_____	$22.00	_____
The Mental Edge	_____	$26.95	_____
Psychology of Winning Notebook	_____	$20.00	_____
Golf Psychology Workbook	_____	$22.00	_____
Mental Edge Clinic Workbook	_____	$25.00	_____
Postage/Handling (Continental US only)		$4.95	_____
(Canada and Foreign Only)		$14.95	_____
Total Amount Due:			_____

Name: _____

Address: _____

City: _____ State: _____ Zip: _____

Home Phone: _____

METHOD OF PAYMENT:

☐ Check enclosed, made payable to **Peak Performance Publishing**

☐ Visa ☐ Mastercard

Card #: _____

Expiration Date: _____

Signature: _____

☐ Please Send Me a FREE Recruiter's Library™ Catalog!

All monies in U.S. Currency Only.

Make check payable to: *Peak Performance Publishing*

and mail to:
Peak Performance Publishing
14728 Shirley Street
Omaha, NE 68144 USA

For Credit Card Orders, Call Toll Free (800) 293-1676

MEET THE *Inside Recruiting*™ STAFF

Steve Brennan

Bridget Ann Weide

Jon Brooks

STEVE BRENNAN is the editor and publisher of *Inside Recruiting*™: *The Master Guide to Successful College Athletic Recruiting.* As President of Peak Performance Consultants, an international education and motivation company based in Omaha, Nebraska, he specializes in motivation, mental preparation and education, and performance enhancement strategies catering to student-athletes, coaches, educators and business people.

Steve has written other coaching-related books which are listed in the Mental Edge Bookstore form on page 170. He is included in the *World Sport Psychology Sourcebook, World Sport Psychology Who's Who, Who's Who in American Education, Two Thousand Notable American Men, Who's Who in the World,* and the *International Who's Who of Business Entrepreneurs.*

Currently, Steve is the executive director of The Recruiters Institute™, the director of The Recruiters Library™, and the founder and executive director of the Midwest Youth Coaches Association. Steve has been a performance consultant with the Kansas City Royals baseball organization and has experience as a basketball analyst on the Creighton University Radio Network.

Steve's clientele includes professional and amateur athletes and coaches, corporate leaders, professional organizations, and all persons striving for peak performance in their lives.

BRIDGET ANN WEIDE provided the layout for *Inside Recruiting*™: **The Master Guide to Successful College Athletic Recruiting.** As co-owner of Image Building Communications in Omaha, Nebraska, Bridget provides writing, editing, layout and design services for a variety of small businesses and organizations in the greater Omaha area. She received her degree in Public Relations from the University of Nebraska at Omaha in 1996. In addition to this book, Bridget produced *The Life and Times of Jesus of Nazareth* by Judd Patton as well as numerous newsletters, journals, and other publications.

JON BROOKS was responsible for editing, cover design, and layout design assistance for *Inside Recruiting*™: **The Master Guide to Successful College Athletic Recruiting.** An avid sports fan, Jon also co-owns Image Building Communications in Omaha, Nebraska. He graduated with honors in 1996 with his degree in Public Relations from the University of Nebraska at Omaha. Jon provides layout and design for numerous newsletters, publications and organizations. He is an editor of *Nebraska Life* magazine.